Literature for the Visual and Performing Arts

Kindergarten Through
Grade Twelve

Publishing Information

Literature for the Visual and Performing Arts, Kindergarten Through Grade Twelve was developed by the History–Social Science and Visual and Performing Arts Office, California Department of Education. The document was edited for publication by Stephanie Prescott, working cooperatively with Diane Brooks and Terry Givens. Jamie Contreras set type for the publication; Carey Johnson created the interior format; and Paul Lee designed and prepared the cover and divider pages.

The document was published by the Department of Education, 721 Capitol Mall, Sacramento, California (mailing address: P.O. Box 944272, Sacramento, CA 94244-2720). It was printed by the Office of State Printing and was distributed under the provisions of the Library Distribution Act and *Government Code* Section 11096.

Copies of this publication are available for $9.50 each—plus shipping and handling charges and, for California residents, sales tax—from the Bureau of Publications, Sales Unit, California Department of Education, P.O. Box 271, Sacramento, CA 95812-0271; FAX (916) 323-0823. For information on shipping and handling charges, call the Sales Unit at (916) 445-1260.

A 64-page illustrated *Educational Resources Catalog,* which describes the content of educational resources available from the Department, can be obtained without charge by writing to the address given above or by calling the Sales Unit at (916) 445-1260.

ISBN 0-8011-1266-4

Cover photograph: *Oak Tree, Snowstorm, Yosemite National Park, 1948,* by Ansel Adams. Copyright © 1995 by the Trustees of the Ansel Adams Publishing Rights Trust. All rights reserved.

One of the greatest photographers of all time, Ansel Adams was also a tireless environmentalist. He used his camera not only to create beautiful photographs but also to plead for the protection of the American wilderness. Students in grades six through eight will enjoy Julie Dunlap's recently published biography of Adams, *Eye on the Wild: A Story About Ansel Adams* (Minneapolis, Minn.: Carolrhoda Books, 1995).

Contents

Foreword

It is art that makes *life, makes interest, makes importance, for our consideration and application of these things, and I know of no substitute whatever for the force and beauty of its process.*

—Henry James, in a letter to H. G. Wells, July 10, 1915

Congratulations! You are about to embark on a glorious adventure into the world of the arts. The resources listed in this publication will provide you and your students with a comprehensive view of the world's great arts traditions. Through these resources, students will enter the life of dancer Margot Fonteyn; they will learn of the importance of Scott Joplin to the heritage of ragtime music; they will become witness to the turmoil and triumph of painter Frida Kahlo; and they will delight in the fantasy of Sir James M. Barrie's wise and witty plays.

The arts embody a culture's most prized ideas and artifacts, its accomplishments as well as its follies. Thus, the architectural and urban remains of the Aztecs speak to us of that civilization's advanced thought and creativity. Such monuments as Trajan's column and the life-size terra-cotta army buried with the Chinese emperor Qin testify, through art, to the self-importance of the men they honor. The more recent engineering and artistic triumph of the Eiffel Tower reflects a merging of art and technology. Indeed, as the President's Committee on the Arts and the Humanities has stated, "The most lasting achievements of past civilizations—whether they be Anasazi, Aztec, Egyptian, Greek, Inca, Indo-Chinese, Japanese, Mayan, Roman, Zulu, or those from any other epoch—can be measured in the arts the people produced, the literature and myths they cherished, and the wisdom they attained."

The stories of the artists, musicians, composers, playwrights, actors, dancers, and choreographers of past and present civilizations come to life through works such as those described on the following pages. Reading these works helps us to reflect on the highest achievements of humankind, to understand the arts and those who use the arts to express themselves, and to become acquainted with the contributions of artists and the arts to humankind. In short, they tell us about why we dream, invent, and long to become better human beings.

Good reading!

Delaine Eastin

State Superintendent of Public Instruction

Preface

At the 1957 opening of the American galleries of the Metropolitan Museum of Art, President Dwight Eisenhower said, "Art is a universal language, and through it each nation makes its own unique contribution to the culture of mankind." How do we study that language so that we, as citizens of the United States, understand the stories of both our common culture and our individual heritage? How do we discover meaning in the languages of the arts so that we understand the unique contributions to civilization made by the American culture and the other cultures of the world? How do we understand the contributions to the American culture made by the cultures which it encompasses?

One of the ways we can begin to comprehend the richness of the language of art is through its literature. Artists speak most directly to us through their works of art: Their creations can inform our own longings, needs, fantasies, dreams, understandings, and expressions. But the stories artists tell and the literature about them and their art can teach us about the sources of inspiration and help us to understand the universal language of the arts.

Literature for the Visual and Performing Arts, Kindergarten Through Grade Twelve was prepared to assist teachers and students in the discovery of the rich cultural and aesthetic tradition to be found in dance, music, theatre, and the visual arts. The books and other resources listed here can lead us and our students on a magical excursion into the imaginations and worlds of great artists, musicians, dancers, and actors. While our life experiences tell us that we are connected to the past through our family traditions and customs, the arts connect us to larger traditions, customs, societies, and cultures. The arts also contribute to literacy. Access to the stories and traditions of the arts of all cultures is an essential component of a comprehensive education, of our understanding of ourselves and others, and of our ability to make thoughtful decisions in a democratic society.

New literary works are being published every day, and older titles go out of print almost as frequently. Consequently, any reading list should be regarded as a "living document," a resource to be expanded as users discover additional appropriate titles. Further, *Literature for the Visual and Performing Arts, Kindergarten Through Grade Twelve* is not intended to be prescriptive. School districts are encouraged to develop and periodically update similar lists based on materials to which they have access.

As this document goes to press, most of the titles listed are obtainable from their publishers. However, works that complement components of the *Framework* or the arts disciplines themselves were not excluded simply because they are no longer in print. Many excellent out-of-print titles are available through school libraries and public library search systems. We hope that our inclusion of books that remain noteworthy for their treatments of the arts, artists, and societies of earlier historical periods will encourage librarians to continue to make these books available in their collections. We also hope, as occurred after the publication of *Literature for History–Social Science, Kindergarten Through Grade Eight* (1991), that publishers will be prompted to make certain titles available once more.

Literature for the Visual and Performing Arts, Kindergarten Through Grade Twelve was developed after lengthy study and research by a large number of teachers, librarians, curriculum specialists, and booksellers. The History–Social Science and Visual and Performing Arts Office is especially grateful to the members of the California Alliance for Arts Education (CAAE), the Legislative Action Coalition for Arts Education (LACAE), the California School Library Association (CSLA), and their constituent organizations. They recommended many selections which they found useful in their own classrooms and provided exceptional advice and criticism. The following consultants in the History–Social Science and Visual and Performing Arts Office helped coordinate the development of this publication over a period of four years: Terry Givens, Miguel Muto, Joan Peterson, and Patty Taylor. Sara Swan, a research assistant, made significant contributions. Mr. Givens also served as principal writer of this publication.

Of particular significance was the support and guidance given to this project by Fred Tempes, who was the Director of the Curriculum, Instruction, and Assessment Division at the time this document was being prepared. His knowledge of the process and his perception and understanding enabled us to avoid many pitfalls that could have grounded us.

The leadership and tenacity of Diane Brooks, Administrator of the History–Social Science and Visual and Performing Arts Office, was invaluable to this project. Without her vision and insight, this publication would not have been possible. Her support of arts programs for all students in all California schools has been a guiding light for us all.

To all of those who assist students in learning the universal language of the arts, appreciating the rich arts heritage, and comprehending through the arts our increasingly complex and heterogeneous society—best wishes for an inspiring, uplifting, and eye-opening excursion.

RUTH MCKENNA
Chief Deputy Superintendent
for Instructional Services

GLEN THOMAS
Assistant Superintendent
and Executive Secretary
Curriculum Commission

PATRICIA HOGAN NEWSOME
Deputy Superintendent
Curriculum and Instructional
Leadership Branch

DIANE L. BROOKS
Administrator
Curriculum Frameworks and
Instructional Resources Unit

Introduction

The Visual and Performing Arts Framework for California Public Schools: Kindergarten Through Grade Twelve discusses two approaches to teaching dance, music, theatre, and the visual arts through the four components of artistic perception, creative expression, historical and cultural contexts, and aesthetic valuing. In the first approach, arts instruction involves students directly in the expressive modes of the arts. That is, students become aware of their own expressive capabilities through the arts. In the second approach, in which the arts are used as a means of acquiring cultural and aesthetic literacy, teachers provide students with opportunities to study aesthetics through analyses of their own and others' responses to works of the arts; to study historical and cultural contexts through the histories of the visual and performing arts and artists; and to become familiar with arts criticism by studying and writing about the arts. Combined, these two approaches take in the vast landscape of the arts in societies over time.

Literature for the Visual and Performing Arts, Kindergarten Through Grade Twelve may be used by those planning or developing curricula in the arts and by classroom teachers and arts specialists. Each of the four sections— "Dance," "Music," "Theatre," and "Visual Arts" —includes an annotated bibliography of resources related to the discipline. An accompanying grid identifies for each title (1) focus of the literature; (2) suggested grade level; (3) related discipline, if applicable; and (4) the relevant *Framework* component.

Using Literature About the Arts in the Classroom

When schools provide ongoing access to books and resources about the arts, children and teachers feel free to use them in a variety of ways: as references for research and stimulation, as sources of enjoyment, and as means of developing literacy.

In 1995 the California Reading Task Force determined that a key element of a balanced and comprehensive approach to reading is a "strong literature, language, and comprehension program that includes a balance of oral and written language."[1] *Literature for the Visual and Performing Arts* is designed to provide assistance in meeting this important goal. Introducing the books listed in each arts discipline section strengthens the oral and written language components of the daily classroom curriculum because the books become access points, not only for the information they convey about the arts but also for the reinforcement they offer of concepts about reading instruction.

Teachers may use supplementary literature about the arts in several ways. One way is to teach the arts—to teach about the intrinsic worth of a particular arts discipline. A second way is to provide a path into the arts discipline. For example, a biography of an artist or a performer, a general history of an artform, or a story may demonstrate how the arts enrich our lives. Literature about the arts may also provide a view into other disciplines, illustrating the interactions between the arts and these disciplines, their parallelisms, or the truths they share. Finally, arts literature provides opportunities for students to learn about other people and other places; about the values and beliefs of others throughout history; and about the influences of the arts and artists on other disciplines and people.

---

[1] *Every Child a Reader: The Report of the California Reading Task Force.* Sacramento: California Department of Education, 1995, p. 1.

Teaching the Arts

Perhaps the most obvious way that literature about the arts can be used in the classroom is in teaching the arts. The uses vary, though, depending on grade level and circumstance. For instance, in a high school theatre class, *Mask Characterization*, by Libby Appel, may help students understand the use of the mask in a production as well as in the training of actors. After students read a play and study its characters, sections of *Mask Characterization* are read aloud or studied by groups of students. Each student or group of students then designs and creates a mask that portrays a character in the selected play. Working with paper maché or cut-paper sculpture, students refer to illustrations in Carol Gelber's *Masks Tell Stories*. Students then perform the play using the expressive masks they have created. Discussions could then take place about the relationships of the masks to the characters themselves. Did the masks enhance the story? Did they make the characterizations more meaningful? What could be done differently to make the masks more of an integral part of the character?

In a fifth grade class, teachers may base a music lesson on Robert Kraus's *Musical Max*, which is about a boy who wants to play a variety of instruments. When studying percussion and rhythm, for example, groups of students follow Max's descriptions to make sets of instruments—such as small and large drums, rattles, and shakers—out of ordinary objects. Then, small groups of students playing either the same or a variety of instruments perform short compositions based on rhythm patterns developed by the teacher. Students use an illustrated songbook, such as *Woody's Twenty Grow-Big Songs*, by Woody Guthrie, to find these rhythm patterns in familiar songs.

Teaching the skills and techniques students need to create or perform artworks is a beginning step in nurturing the creative process. To deepen their artistic experiences, students also need to find meaning in them. This search for meaning connects them with feelings which they express through the arts. When students create the expressive masks mentioned earlier, they discuss not only how but also why they created their masks as they did. Their experiences with art allow them to use a variety of ways to communicate with their peers and the rest of the world.

Providing a Path Into the Arts

Using *A Painter*, by Douglas Florian, the first or second grade teacher introduces students to what a painter does and what he or she feels and thinks about while painting. The teacher reads the story aloud and shows the illustrations to the students. Students then react to the story by telling about the subjects they would like to draw or paint, the sizes of the compositions they would like to create, and the media they want to use. Since these three characteristics of a painting are identified in the story, the teacher reminds students about them. The students' suggestions are listed on the chalkboard as students mention them. Students then choose one item from each list and make paintings or drawings that incorporate the selected elements.

Students in a high school dance class study *Mikhail Baryshnikov*, by Bruce Glassman, to understand Baryshnikov's impact on the world of contemporary dance. Students have been studying classical ballet technique and are moving into the development of their own style and choreography. After a field trip to a ballet rehearsal that includes a discussion of the rehearsal with the dancers and the choreographer, students write journal entries that reflect the influence of Baryshnikov on the ballet rehearsal they viewed. Then they work in small groups to create a dance based on a specific theme, emphasizing the contrast between classical ballet and contemporary dance movement.

Using literature such as *A Painter* and *Mikhail Baryshnikov* as a path into the arts helps students become engaged in the arts through another artistic medium. As part of a balanced, comprehensive program of literacy, reading to students and encouraging them to read books about the arts promotes their awareness of aesthetic experiences.[2] Such literature gives students a brief look at an artist, a performer, an artistic event, or a performance. As students themselves create or perform, they are reminded of major artists' and performers' means of infusing meaning into their creations and performances. The aesthetic experience is, in part, a search for meaning; students need to be encouraged to find and create meaning in their own lives.

Viewing Another Discipline Through the Arts

Seventh graders studying the history–social science unit on China use *The Terra Cotta Army of Emperor Qin,* by Caroline Lazo, to explore the context and culture of an ancient civilization.[3] This book provides a beginning point for the *History–Social Science Framework* unit "Connecting with Past Learnings: Uncovering the Remote Past." It could also be used in grade six, in the unit "West Meets East: The Early Civilizations of India and China." After reading about the discovery of the terra-cotta figures, the class studies the location in which they were found and the ways in which an archaeologist works. Using slides taken from Lazo's book or another source, students write about the differences and similarities between the Chinese terra-cotta figures and Greek funerary steles. They work in small, heterogeneous groups to determine a rationale for the placement of the figures, to trace the myths and legends each form represents, and to summarize their perceptions of the Chinese culture. By emphasizing intense scrutiny and description of artwork, teachers encourage students to explore its nature and its integral connection to culture. Students' previous experiences in writing about other objects relating to art and culture aid them in this activity.

That's a Wrap, by Ned Dowd, is used in an eighth grade literature class to expand student writing. This supplementary text examines the behind-the-scenes activity in the production of a motion picture. It covers script writing, preproduction tasks, filming, and postproduction activities. The teacher reads sections of this book to the class and shows overhead transparencies made from selected pages of the book. Students then work in small groups to write scripts for drama productions to be given in class. Included in their scripts are instructions for characterization, costuming, sets, and stage directions. After each group of students presents its production, students write critical analyses using skills studied earlier.

Tar Beach, by Faith Ringgold, is used in a fourth or fifth grade class to provide opportunities for students to become personally involved in a story through the illustrations, or vice versa. In this story, illustrated by the author, a young girl flies over her neighborhood, identifying and laying claim to all she sees. Personal involvement allows students to appreciate both the story and the illustrations, understand more about the life of the artist, and read a book about art in a way that becomes an aesthetic experience.

Those who use this document will discover that some books listed as appropriate for one arts discipline may be used in other disciplines as well. For example, Carol Gelber's *Masks Tell Stories* conveys the significance of masks in societies from their use in tribal ceremonies, the theatre, and even everyday life. This book is listed in the "Theatre" section but could very easily be used by a visual arts teacher to examine the heritage of the artform when developing a unit in mask making.

---

[2] See *Every Child a Reader,* p. 7.

[3] See Unit VI, "China," in COURSE MODELS FOR THE HISTORY–SOCIAL SCIENCE FRAMEWORK, GRADE SEVEN—*World History and Geography: Medieval and Early Modern Times.* Sacramento: California Department of Education, 1994.

Masks Tell Stories could also be used in a dance lesson to illustrate the uses of dance in celebrations. *Ragtime Tumpie*, written by Alan Schroeder, also is appropriate for more than one category. This fictionalized story of Josephine Baker tells of her dreams of escaping her life on Gratiot Street in the poorest section of the vivacious, ragtime, turn-of-the-century St. Louis to become a famous dancer. While this book is listed in the music section, its luminous illustrations by Bernie Fuchs could be used in a visual arts lesson.

Whatever the material, the criteria for identifying and using books are the four components articulated in the *Visual and Performing Arts Framework:* artistic perception, creative expression, historical and cultural context, and aesthetic valuing. If students are to learn the arts in a balanced way, through each of these components, the curriculum development process must ensure the careful selection of materials.

Books about the arts need to be part of every classroom library. The report of the California Reading Task Force, *Every Child a Reader,* recommends that "classroom libraries should be used to encourage students to read and write in class and at home" (p. 10). Classroom libraries provide easy access to the richness of literature about the arts. As noted in the next section of this publication, "Meeting Students' Special Needs," students need to read about subjects that engage their interest. Many of the books in this publication are appropriate for students who are learning to read. By engaging their interest in the paintings of children, music about nursery rhymes, the drama of folktales, and dance that expresses joy, students connect the skills of reading to real and imagined aspects of their own lives. For students reading to learn, literature about artists—dancers struggling for new ways to express their ideas and feelings; playwrights using their own experiences in their scripts; musicians learning to communicate ideas and emotions to audiences; and artists expressing their ideas in new media—helps them connect their own learning to the struggles of people everywhere who are learning or trying new things.

Meeting Students' Special Needs

Students in programs under Title I of the Improving America's Schools Act (IASA) must be provided with a rich core curriculum. It is the responsibility of the local district to provide instruction in the arts to all students as part of this curriculum. The disciplines which make up arts education provide a depth of content that is ideal for instructing students who have special needs:

> For the language arts to function, they must be applied to some content. All students learn to listen by attending to that which edifies. They learn to talk not only by talking but also by talking about something substantive. They learn to read by reading something which engages their interest and fulfills a purpose and to write by composing that which records or clarifies.[4]

The arts function as a common language that cuts across cultures and verbal communication. Each of the arts disciplines—dance, music, theatre, and the visual arts—has its own symbol system and syntax. Each creates its own metaphors through its basic elements and their interaction and communicates in its own form. Once students learn the language through the various methods developed by experts in the field, their experience with the literature listed in this publication will heighten their aesthetic sensitivity and their appreciation of the arts. Faithful translations of major

---

[4] *Effective Language Arts Programs for Chapter 1 and Migrant Education Students.* Sacramento: California Department of Education, 1989, p. 5.

works of literature about the arts would make it possible for students to grasp content as they are developing English fluency. Trade book publishers are encouraged to consider this potential market.

The reader is also referred to *With History–Social Science for All: Access for Every Student*, published by the California Department of Education (1992). This publication addresses special considerations in planning history–social science programs that meet diverse educational needs, including those of students in migrant education and Title I programs. Even though this publication deals with history–social science, many examples integrate the arts, and other teaching strategies can be translated by teachers into lessons and units concerning the arts. *With History–Social Science for All* proposes six strategies for ensuring access to the curriculum for all students. One strategy is to connect history to other learnings. In one example, students study history through art by focusing on the Harlem Renaissance: "During the Jazz Age, blacks who were visual artists, poets, philosophers, novelists, dramatists, and musicians contributed to an artistic and intellectual outpouring that established Harlem as the international capital of African-American culture. This movement, the Harlem Renaissance, was spearheaded by W. E. B. Du Bois, Alain Locke, and Langston Hughes."[5] The arts of this period may "capture the curiosity of otherwise disinterested students," and "connect" them to the history curriculum. By reading *Duke Ellington,* by James Lincoln Collier, for example, students learn about the effects of Ellington's music on the society of the Harlem Renaissance. The Cotton Club, where Ellington played for many years, had a major influence on the culture of the time. Students can explore that era through its music and musicians.

Another strategy suggested by *With History–Social Science for All* is connecting history to personal experience. Thus, an analysis might include works of the student's own family members, works by individuals within the student's community, or works by those with whom the student initiates correspondence. In *The Quilt Story,* by Tony Johnston and Tomie DePaola, a young frontier girl reflects on her patchwork quilt and its transformation through the generations of her family. A student reading this book could use it as the basis for an exploration of his or her own cultural and family artifacts over years and their effects on family memories.

Another strategy is to have students learn history by studying peoples' lives. Biographies such as those listed in this document reveal to students how an artist's background influences the works he or she produces. The society, in turn, is affected by the work the artist creates; this influence is also demonstrated through a careful reading of the biographies. In *Elvis Presley: The Rise of Rock and Roll*, by David Rubel, students from grade six to grade twelve can read how popular music and, indeed, popular culture itself, were changed through the music and style created by this musician and performer.

When the curriculum touches students' lives and speaks to them personally through anecdotes, stories, and other expressions of art and literature, students' inclination to learn is heightened. This bibliography of resources on the arts and artists identifies those kinds of magical touchstones.

Classifying the Literature

Each resource cited in the lists to follow is categorized as to its subject matter or genre; the grade level or levels for which it is appropriate; other disciplines to which it applies; and the component or components articulated in the *Visual and Performing Arts Framework,* which it supports. Resources on videotape or film are identified by the ✪ symbol before the title.

---

[5] *With History–Social Science for All: Access for Every Student.* Sacramento: California Department of Education, 1992, p. 17.

Focus of the Literature

Six categories of literature are identified and, in many cases, more than one classification may be applied to a title. Descriptions of the classifications and their abbreviations as used in the lists follow:

Arts of world cultures (WC)

These books describe how the arts are used in celebrations, analyze their functions in a society, and often define their symbolism. Some books, such as *The Art of Ancient Peru,* by Shirley Glubok, focus on the arts in a specific historical period. Others, such as *The Wonderful Chirrionera and Other Tales from Mexican Folklore,* by David Lindsey, include folktales which could be used in classroom drama activities.

Stories about the arts (S)

Adventures, fantasies, historical tales, dreams, and aspirations about the arts are included in this category. For example, Denise Lewis Patrick's book *Red Dancing Shoes* tells what happens when a young girl receives a pair of red dancing shoes from her grandmother. In *Suho and the White Horse,* Yuzo Otsuka recounts an ancient Mongolian folktale about the ennobling power of music.

Techniques and skills in the arts (T)

Books in this category focus on learning the skills necessary to produce artworks. Philip Yenawine's *Stories* and *Colors,* for example, use works of modern visual art to sharpen skills of perception. *On Their Toes: A Russian Ballet School,* by Ann Morris, describes the training a dancer must undertake. Teachers can use these books to demonstrate the persistence and practice necessary to understand the arts or pursue a career as an artist.

Collections of works about the arts (C)

This category includes general collections of works of art, such as Neil Waldman's *America the Beautiful.* This illustrated edition of the nineteenth-century poem (later set to music), features paintings by Waldman. This category also includes *Ballet Stories,* by Joan Lawson, a collection of stories about favorite ballets, and *Out of the Blue: Poems About Color,* by Hiawyn Oram, a collection for primary students.

Histories of the arts (H)

These books range from very specific histories, such as *Black Music in America: A History Through Its People,* by James Haskins, to general works, such as *The Magic Lantern: How Movies Got to Move,* a history of early moviemaking, by Judith Thurman and David Jonathan.

Biographies and autobiographies (B)

Books in this category often provide students with the easiest and most interesting access to a subject. *Introducing Michelangelo,* by Robin Richmond, presents examples of Michelangelo's work along with his life story. Agnes de Mille's autobiography, *Dance to the Piper,* highlights both the technical training and the awakening of artistic sensibilities of a young dancer. *Charlie Parker Played Be-Bop,* by Chris Raschka, through its exciting design and layout, introduces primary students to the rhythm and excitement of jazz.

Grade Level

Grade-level suggestions are simply that. Many of the books can be used by older or younger students than those in the grades identified, and teachers are encouraged to interpret these designations loosely. If the topic is appropriate, but the reading level is too difficult, all or portions of a book may be read aloud by the teacher or an older student. Many picture books designed for younger students may be enjoyed or used by older students as research sources or as prompts in the creative process. For instance, *Ragtime Tumpie,* by Alan Schroeder, is suggested for grades four and five, but this story of Josephine Baker could be used by middle school teachers to begin a study about the effects of poverty and racism in the United States, one of which has been the migration of many black entertainers to Europe. The illustrations by Bernie Fuchs may be used in a high school visual arts class to demonstrate various painting techniques and to stimulate discussion about composition and design.

Related Discipline

When appropriate, a resource's connection to another discipline is indicated. For instance, *Eugenio,* by Marianne Cockenpot, may be easily integrated with English–language arts. Through the title character, who is raised by circus performers, students get a glimpse of circus life. *Eugenio* could be used as the basis for classroom drama exercises as well as for writing exercises in which children propose different endings to the story or analyze different components of the story, such as the characters, plot, or setting. *Just a Dream,* by Chris Van Allsburg, is referenced to science because it can stimulate a discussion about ecological concerns, and students can study its stunning illustrations.

Framework Component

The last column in the grid identifies the component, as articulated in the *Visual and Performing Arts Framework: Kindergarten Through Grade Twelve,* that each resource supports. Although more than one component may be relevant in any citation, only the predominant component is identified. The teacher may use any resource to support components other than the one identified, if appropriate. The following descriptions of these components are adapted from those that appear in the *Framework*:

Artistic perception (AP)

Artistic perception can be defined as the processing of sensory information through elements unique to the arts. Each art is essential in the curriculum because of the particular avenues of artistic perception that it develops.

Increased artistic perception sensitizes the individual to the world. As one develops a fuller awareness of the nuances of light, color, sound, movement, and composition through experiences in the arts, otherwise ordinary perception takes on an artistic dimension. Heightened artistic perception provides a stimulus for imagination and creativity and has the potential to enhance all learning. The development of artistic perception enables one to comprehend and respond to the essential elements of an object or event and to describe and appreciate it in greater depth and detail.

Artistic perception is at the heart of subject-centered instruction, since it provides students with the basic knowledge and skills necessary to communicate in each art form. It is also a process through which the vocabulary of aesthetic valuing is developed.

Creative expression (CE)

Creative expression refers to producing artworks, either by creating them or performing the works of others. Expression in the arts includes the doing of the arts—performing dance styles such as ballet, modern dance, and jazz, folk, and social dancing; singing and playing instruments, alone and in ensembles; acting in plays and improvisations; and creating paintings, ceramic pots, sculpture, and masks.

Direct personal involvement in these expressive modes is necessary if one is to understand and appreciate each discipline. Purposeful arts activities focus, channel, and encourage communication and originality while enhancing understanding of the structure and language of the arts. In creative expression, the artistic perception appropriate to each art is embodied in concrete objects and performances.

The emphasis in creative expression is on the process of creating as well as on the product, for an important aspect of creative expression in arts education is understanding how art is made. Creative experiences foster problem solving and divergent thinking and promote originality, imagination, and creativity.

Historical and cultural context (HCC)

Historical and cultural contexts refer to the time and place in which an artwork was made. The study of the arts within cultural contexts develops a broad base for students to understand artists, their works, their processes, the effects their society and times had on them, and their effects on society. A knowledge of the artistic accomplishments of world cultures enables students to see the importance of the arts in relation to those cultures and to grasp the relevance of the arts in contemporary society. Knowledge of the arts of various cultures, past and present, helps students appreciate and understand these cultures and their own heritage.

Students working on their own art productions or performances connect their work to that of artists in other times and places. Their research involves visiting libraries and museums; viewing slide collections, reenactments and re-creations of historic events, and videotaped performances; and listening to audiotaped performances. Through their research they gain the confidence that comes from making connections with great traditions and the critical judgment that comes from comparing their work to that of both predecessors and contemporaries.

Aesthetic valuing (AV)

Aesthetic valuing means analyzing, making informed judgments, and pursuing meaning in the arts. Aesthetic valuing originates in a branch of philosophy called aesthetics, which is concerned with the nature of beauty, art, and taste. To develop aesthetic sensibilities, students focus on the sensory, intellectual, emotional, and philosophic bases for understanding the arts and for making judgments about their forms, contents, techniques, and purposes. Through study, reflection, and direct experience, students develop criteria for making personal judgments and formulating a personal aesthetic which they can apply throughout their lives for fulfilling experiences in the arts.

This process of developing judgment, commonly called criticism, is the foundation of public discussion about the merit of works of creative expression. Being able to criticize justly, to value a work aesthetically, means applying knowledge of the other three *Framework* components in light of the work being contemplated.

Dance

	Focus	Grade level	Related discipline	Framework component
Ackerman, Karen. *Song and Dance Man.* New York: Knopf, 1989.	S	K–3	E–LA	AP
When Grandpa's grandchildren follow him up the attic stairs, a dazzling show begins. Grandpa opens a dusty trunk, pulls out a bowler hat and gold-tipped cane, and suddenly the children are back in the days of the song-and-dance vaudeville shows. Grandpa brings to life the old soft-shoe routines.				
Anderson, Joan. *Twins on Toes: A Ballet Debut.* New York: Dutton, 1993.	S	4–5	E–LA	AP
Twins Amy and Laurel Foster trained for ten years to become professional ballerinas and studied at the School of American Ballet. The large color photographs enhance the text.				
Arnold, Sandra M. *Alicia Alonso: First Lady of the Ballet.* New York: Walker and Company, 1993.	B	6–8	H–SS	HCC
This biography of the Cuban-born dancer, one of the premier ballerinas during the early days of the American Ballet Theatre, recounts her promising youth, virtual blindness in her early twenties, and subsequent career. She continues to dance and inspire.				
Balanchine, George, and Francis Mason. *101 Stories of the Great Ballets.* New York: Anchor, 1989.	H	9–12		HCC AV
Written by the world's most renowned choreographer, ballet master, and teacher, this collection presents scene-by-scene stories of 101 popular ballets.				
Barboza, Steven. *I Feel Like Dancing: A Year with d'Amboise and the National Dance Institute.* New York: Crown, 1992.	H	4–5		AP HCC
The experiences of students during the year they spent as members of Jacques d'Amboise's National Dance Institute are described in text and photographs. The photographs vividly show the exuberance of both d'Amboise and his students.				
Brady, Joan. *The Unmaking of a Dancer.* New York: Washington Square Press, 1992.	B	9–12		AV
This is the true story of a brave woman's hard-won victory over fear and failure—a woman who, against all odds, proved to herself and to the world that vanished dreams can be brought to life.				
Brighton, Catherine. *Nijinsky: Scenes from the Childhood of the Great Dancer.* New York: Doubleday, 1989.	B	6–8	H–SS	HCC
This vivid biography describes how the renowned Russian ballet dancer found an outlet for his childhood unhappiness through dance and was eventually called to perform for the tsar.				

Focus: B—Biography and autobiography; **C**—Collection of works; **H**—History; **S**—Story; **T**—Techniques or skills; **WC**—World cultures
Related discipline: D—Dance; **E–LA**—English–language arts; **H–SS**—History–social science; **MA**—Mathematics; **MU**—Music; **S**—Science; **TH**—Theatre; **VA**—Visual arts
Framework component: AP—Artistic perception; **AV**—Aesthetic valuing; **CE**—Creative expression; **HCC**—Historical and cultural context

○ Denotes film or videotape

	Focus	Grade level	Related discipline	Framework component
Bussell, Darcey. *The Young Dancer.* New York: Dorling Kindersley, 1994. The importance of mastering basic steps early and building strength slowly are explained in this large-format book. Also included are fascinating information about ballet companies, useful addresses, and a photographic glossary of ballet terms.	T	6–8		HCC AV
Careers for People Who Like to Perform. Edited by Russell Shorto. Brookfield, Conn.: Millbrook, 1994. People working in a wide range of performing careers, including dance, music, acting, and juggling, are highlighted in this illustrated book.	B	4–5	H–SS TH	AP HCC
Carlson, Nancy. *Harriet's Recital.* New York: Reading Rainbow Book, 1988. Harriet, a dancing bear, anxiously prepares for her first dance recital. She is surprised when everything goes well.	S	K–3	E–LA	AP
Cheney, Gay. *Basic Concepts in Modern Dance: A Creative Approach* (Third edition). Pennington, N.J.: Princeton Book Company, 1989. The author discusses modern dance and movement, the body as instrument, abstract elements of dance, choreography, performance, self-evaluation, and the dance experience.	H	9–12		AP AV
Chwanec, Audrey. *Tutu.* New York: Sutton, 1991. Bright illustrations accompany a young ballerina's discovery of the care and precision that go into making a tutu. The author concludes with a history of the tutu in ballet.	H	K–3	E–LA	AP HCC
Cosi, Liliana. *The Young Ballet Dancer.* New York: Stein and Day, 1979. Enhanced with illustrations, this book details the training for both male and female dancers. The history and stories of some famous ballets are also recounted.	H	4–5		AP HCC
Daly, Niki. *Papa Lucky's Shadow.* New York: McElderry, 1992. Nestled upon her grandfather's lap, Sugar listens happily to stories about the days when he could "dance the sequins off a champ." This warm, intergenerational story is flavored with a bit of nostalgia. Daly's illustrations are filled with movement and rhythm.	S	K–3	E–LA	AV
The Dance Has Many Faces (Third edition). Edited by Walter Sorrel. Chicago: A cappella Books, 1992. This unique and insightful collection includes essays by George Balanchine, Frederick Ashton, Doris Humphrey, Charles Weidman, Erick Hawkins, Pauline Koner, and leading African-American choreographers.	H	9–12	H–SS E–LA	HCC

Focus: B—Biography and autobiography; **C**—Collection of works; **H**—History; **S**—Story; **T**—Techniques or skills; **WC**—World cultures
Related discipline: D—Dance; **E–LA**—English–language arts; **H–SS**—History–social science; **MA**—Mathematics; **MU**—Music; **S**—Science; **TH**—Theatre; **VA**—Visual arts
Framework **component: AP**—Artistic perception; **AV**—Aesthetic valuing; **CE**—Creative expression; **HCC**—Historical and cultural context
✪ Denotes film or videotape

	Focus	Grade level	Related discipline	Framework component
de Mille, Agnes. *Dance to the Piper.* New York: Da Capo, 1950 (1980 reprint). Ms. de Mille's autobiography, written in an engaging, anecdotal style, highlights both the technical training and the awakening of artistic sensibilities of the young dancer.	B	9–12	H–SS E–LA	HCC
Dickens, Lucy. *Dancing Class.* New York: Viking, 1992. A little girl learns that dance can serve as an outlet for creativity and self-expression. Movement games and exercises are illustrated with the author's bright paintings.	S	K–3	E–LA	AP
Donohue, Shiobhan. *Kristi Yamaguchi: Artist on Ice.* New York: Lerner, 1994. This biography of the figure skater who won the National, Olympic, and World Championships in 1992 discusses Ms. Yamaguchi's early career and her influences.	B	4–5	H–SS	HCC
☢ *An Evening with the Alvin Ailey American Dance Theatre.* RM Arts, n.d. Choreography by Judith Jamison, Talley Beatty, and Alvin Ailey. Order from HomeVision, 5547 N. Ravenswood Avenue, Chicago, IL 60640-1199, (800) 826-3456. In this studio recording, one of the country's boldest dance companies displays its distinctive style: dazzling, brash, dynamic, yet graceful and poetic. Included are performances of *Divining: The Stack-Up; Revelations;* and *Cry.*	B	9–12	D	HCC
Ewing, William. *Breaking Bounds.* San Francisco: Chronicle Books, 1992. Lois Greenfield's dance photography between 1982 and 1991 broke new ground. Ewing interviews Greenfield and presents her career through her photographs.	B	9–12	VA	AV
Fonteyn, Margot, and Trina Schart Hyman. *Swan Lake.* New York: Gulliver Books, 1989. This beautifully illustrated tale of the classic ballet *Swan Lake* is told by one of the greatest ballerinas of our time. She concludes with a history of the ballet and its significance for dancers throughout the world.	S	4–5	E–LA H–SS	HCC
French, Vivian, and Jan Ormerod. *One Ballerina Two.* New York: Lothrop, Lee and Shepard, 1991. This counting book is illustrated with pictures of two young girls performing ballet exercises. The young girls often mirror each other, but they also show their own individuality.	S	K–3		AP

Focus: B—Biography and autobiography; **C**—Collection of works; **H**—History; **S**—Story; **T**—Techniques or skills; **WC**—World cultures
Related discipline: D—Dance; **E–LA**—English–language arts; **H–SS**—History–social science; **MA**—Mathematics; **MU**—Music; **S**—Science; **TH**—Theatre; **VA**—Visual arts
Framework **component: AP**—Artistic perception; **AV**—Aesthetic valuing; **CE**—Creative expression; **HCC**—Historical and cultural context

☢ Denotes film or videotape

	Focus	Grade level	Related discipline	Framework component
Gabriele-Wosien, Maria. *Sacred Dance.* New York: Thames and Hudson, 1986.	WC	9–12		HCC
This historical overview shows that dance is a vital part of religious traditions in cultures around the world.				
Garfunkel, Trudy. *Letter to the World: The Life and Dances of Martha Graham.* Boston: Little, Brown, 1995.	B	4–5		HCC
One of America's most inspirational and successful dancers and choreographers, Graham redefined the nature of dance and choreography. This biography sketches her life from her apprenticeship with the Denishawn group to her death at age ninety-six.				
Garfunkel, Trudy. *On Wings of Joy: The Story of Ballet from the Sixteenth Century to Today.* Boston: Little, Brown, 1994.	H	6–8		HCC
This history of ballet begins, in a chapter titled "Overture," by stating that "Dance may be the oldest art form" and continues with the influences of Catherine de' Medici and Louis XIV.				
Gauch, Patricia Lee. *Bravo, Tanya.* New York: Philomel, 1992.	S	K–3	E–LA	AP
Tanya loves to dance, but she has trouble integrating her steps with the clapping and counting of her ballet teacher until she tries moving to the music and the sounds inside her head. The watercolor illustrations by Satomi Ichikawa beautifully complement the text.				
Giannini, Enzo. *Zorina Ballerina.* New York: Simon and Schuster, 1993.	S	K–3	E–LA	AV
In this story, based on a factual collaboration between Balanchine and Stravinsky in 1942, Zorina, a very young circus elephant, dreams of "the glamorous life of a prima ballerina." A famous Russian ballet master arrives to teach the elephants the polka.				
Glassman, Bruce. *Mikhail Baryshnikov.* Englewood Cliffs, N.J.: Silver Burdett, 1990.	B	6–8	H–SS	HCC
This biography of the brilliant ballet dancer describes how he went on to become a choreographer, film actor, and director of the American Ballet Theatre.				
Graham, Martha. *Blood Memory.* New York: Doubleday, 1991.	B	9–12		HCC
This is Martha Graham's own account of her life and career from 1894 to 1991. Regarded as the most important and influential American dancer ever born, she broke traditional molds and created new forms of expression, changing the way we look at the world.				

Focus: B—Biography and autobiography; **C**—Collection of works; **H**—History; **S**—Story; **T**—Techniques or skills; **WC**—World cultures
Related discipline: D—Dance; **E–LA**—English–language arts; **H–SS**—History–social science; **MA**—Mathematics; **MU**—Music; **S**—Science; **TH**—Theatre; **VA**—Visual arts
Framework **component: AP**—Artistic perception; **AV**—Aesthetic valuing; **CE**—Creative expression; **HCC**—Historical and cultural context

○ Denotes film or videotape

	Focus	Grade level	Related discipline	Framework component
Harns, J.; A. Pittman; and M. Waller. *Dance Awhile* (Sixth edition). New York: Macmillan, 1988. Genres such as American square dance, international folk dance, ballroom dance, and contra dance are described and illustrated in this collection. Good background information is provided for some of the more difficult dances.	T	4–5	H–SS E–LA	AP CE
Haskins, James. *Black Dance in America: A History Through Its People.* New York: HarperTrophy, 1990. This survey traces black dance in America from its beginnings in the ritual dances of African slaves, through tap and modern dance, to break dancing. Brief biographies of influential dancers and companies are included.	H	9–12	H–SS E–LA	HCC
Hawkins, Alma. *Creating Through Dance* (Revised edition). Pennington, N.J.: Princeton Book Company, 1988. This book, on the development of dance, touches on aesthetics, movement, and dance composition.	T	9–12		AP HCC
Hill, Elizabeth Starr. *Broadway Chances.* New York: Puffin, 1992. In this sequel to *The Street Dancers,* also by Elizabeth Starr Hill, twelve-year-old Fritzi, finally settled into a normal life after years of street performances with her parents, gets a chance to star in a Broadway musical.	S	6–8	E–LA	HCC AV
Hoff, Bernard. *Duncan the Dancing Duck.* New York: Houghton Mifflin, 1994. Duncan is a duckling who dances his way from the pond to international stardom. After experiencing the limelight, he's exhausted and returns home to "swim, swim, swim with his family." Vivid colors enhance Hoff's typical, stylized cartoons.	S	K–3	E–LA	AV
Hollinshead, Marilyn. *The Nine Days Wonder.* New York: Putnam, 1994. Will Kemp, a contemporary of Shakespeare and an actor in many of the Bard's plays, was also a dancer of jigs. In 1601 he vowed to dance his way from London to Norwich. Hollinshead has taken this historical event and turned it into a fictional romp.	S	4–5	E–LA	HCC
Humphrey, Doris. *The Art of Making Dances.* New York: Grove, 1959. This classic presents modern dance as theatre. It contains a short history of the dance, and various chapters discuss the design, dynamics, and rhythm of dance. Many recent editions are available in paperback.	T	9–12		AP CE

Focus: B—Biography and autobiography; **C**—Collection of works; **H**—History; **S**—Story; **T**—Techniques or skills; **WC**—World cultures

Related discipline: D—Dance; **E–LA**—English–language arts; **H–SS**—History–social science; **MA**—Mathematics; **MU**—Music; **S**—Science; **TH**—Theatre; **VA**—Visual arts

Framework **component: AP**—Artistic perception; **AV**—Aesthetic valuing; **CE**—Creative expression; **HCC**—Historical and cultural context

✪ Denotes film or videotape

	Focus	Grade level	Related discipline	Framework component
Jamison, Judith. *Dancing Spirit*. New York: Anchor, 1993. This is a powerful testimony by a dancer and choreographer that discipline and determination can foster great achievements. Jamison describes her life and challenges readers to recognize their own gifts, develop them, and excel.	B	9–12		HCC AV
Jonas, Ann. *Color Dance*. New York: Greenwillow, 1989. This joyous book shows with photographs of the movements and costumes of young dancers how colors mix and combine. Primary and secondary colors combine to create combinations when dancers coordinate their movements in a variety of ways.	S	K–3	VA	AP CE
Jonas, Gerald. *Dancing*. New York: Harry Abrams, 1994. *Dancing* is the companion volume to the eight-part series made for public television. The focus is on the fact that dance is found in all human societies. Carefully selected examples of great dance traditions are explored to illuminate the many functions dance performs in cultures around the world.	WC	9–12		HCC
Kerner, Mary. *Barefoot to Balanchine*. New York: Doubleday, 1991. There are many facets of dance, and Kerner successfully describes each one of them in this book. The author illuminates everything seen on the stage and shows how to get the most out of watching dance performances.	H	9–12		AV
King, Sandra. *Shannon: An Ojibway Dancer*. Minneapolis, Minn.: Lerner, 1993. Shannon, who lives in Minneapolis with her grandmother, sisters, and cousins, is a fancy shawl dancer. Snippets of family conversation in each book lend an intimacy and familiarity not usually available to non-Indian readers. This book is illustrated with photographs by Native American photographers.	S	4–5	H–SS	HCC
Kirkland, Gelsey. *Dancing on My Grave*. New York: Jove Books, 1987. The autobiography of Gelsey Kirkland, a prima ballerina who danced with George Balanchine and the New York City Ballet, traces her struggle for ambition and great talent and reveals the glory and pain it brought her.	B	9–12		HCC
Klosty, James. *Merce Cunningham*. New York: Proscenium Publications, 1986. A celebration of Merce Cunningham in words and photographs, this book documents the central place he occupies in the world of dance and in the avant-garde of the visual and performing arts of the modern era.	B	9–12		HCC

Focus: **B**—Biography and autobiography; **C**—Collection of works; **H**—History; **S**—Story; **T**—Techniques or skills; **WC**—World cultures
Related discipline: **D**—Dance; **E–LA**—English–language arts; **H–SS**—History–social science; **MA**—Mathematics; **MU**—Music; **S**—Science; **TH**—Theatre; **VA**—Visual arts
Framework component: **AP**—Artistic perception; **AV**—Aesthetic valuing; **CE**—Creative expression; **HCC**—Historical and cultural context

❂ Denotes film or videotape

	Focus	Grade level	Related discipline	Framework component
Krementz, Jill. *A Very Young Dancer.* New York: Knopf, 1976. Excellent photographs enhance this story of a young girl's preparation to appear in a production of *The Nutcracker.*	S	K–3	E–LA	AP HCC
Kukin, Susan. *Going to My Ballet Class.* New York: Bradbury, 1989. Photographs accompany a young girl's description of what she does in her ballet class. Also included is information about how to choose a ballet class for young children.	S	K–3	E–LA	AP
Laubin, Reginald, and Gladys Laubin. *Indian Dancers of North America—Their Importance to Indian Life.* Norman: University of Oklahoma Press, 1989. The authors convey the deeply spiritual import of American Indian dance and present cultural background material. Included are a brief survey of principal tribal dance forms and a section on specific tribal dances.	H	9–12	H–SS	HCC AV
Lawson, Joan. *Ballet Stories.* New York: Mayflower, 1979. Lawson retells the stories of 14 favorite ballets, including *Giselle* and the major works by Tchaikovsky.	C	4–5	E–LA	HCC
Lee, Jeanne. *Silent Lotus.* New York: Farrar, Straus and Giroux, 1991. Inspired by the twelfth-century temple at Angkor Wat, the author tells a tale from long-ago Kampuchea (Cambodia). Young Lotus, deaf and unable to speak from birth, learns to communicate with her hands and becomes a dancer at the king's palace, telling her stories with her graceful gestures.	WC	K–3	E–LA	HCC AV
Levine, Ellen. *Anna Pavlova: Genius of the Dance.* New York: Scholastic, 1995. This biography will appeal to dancers and to anyone interested in the arts, women's studies, and early twentieth-century world history. A delightful work, it is full of the energy and charm that was Pavlova.	B	6–8	H–SS	HCC
Louis, Murray. *Inside Dance.* New York: St. Martin's, 1981. This is a charming and funny account of various aspects of the backstage life of a modern dancer at home and on the road.	S	9–12	E–LA	AP
McMullan, Kate. *Nutcracker Noel.* New York: HarperCollins, 1993. Noel wants to land the starring role in *The Nutcracker,* but instead she gets to be a tree. She tries every trick in the book to get a better part, but on opening night one of life's little surprises turns Noel's tree into the star. Wonderful illustrations are provided by Jim McMullan.	S	4–5	H–SS	AP HCC

Focus: B—Biography and autobiography; **C**—Collection of works; **H**—History; **S**—Story; **T**—Techniques or skills; **WC**—World cultures
Related discipline: D—Dance; **E–LA**—English–language arts; **H–SS**—History–social science; **MA**—Mathematics; **MU**—Music; **S**—Science;
  TH—Theatre; **VA**—Visual arts
Framework **component: AP**—Artistic perception; **AV**—Aesthetic valuing; **CE**—Creative expression; **HCC**—Historical and cultural context

◯ Denotes film or videotape

	Focus	Grade level	Related discipline	Framework component
✪ *The Margot Fonteyn Story.* RM Arts, n.d. Order from HomeVision, 5547 N. Ravenswood Avenue, Chicago, IL 60640-1199, (800) 826-3456. For four decades Margot Fonteyn thrilled audiences worldwide. For the first time on video, Fonteyn tells her life story; candid revelations are augmented by archival film and interviews.	B	9–12	VA	HCC
Marshall, James. *The Cut-Ups Carry On.* New York: Viking, 1990. Cut-ups Spud and Joe find themselves enrolled in a dance class, but a dance contest brings out their fun and creativity. The humorous story is enhanced by Marshall's cartoon characters as it unfolds.	S	K–3	E–LA	AP
Martin, Bill, and John Archambault. *Barn Dance!* New York: Holt, 1986. Under the light of a full moon, a skinny kid creeps from his bedroom to join a fiddling scarecrow and the farm animals in a merry barn dance. Evocative watercolors add to the spirit.	S	K–3	E–LA	AP
Mazo, Joseph H. *Prime Movers.* New York: William Morrow, 1977. The author introduces modern dance pioneers, such as Lori Fuller, Isadora Duncan, Ruth St. Denis, Ted Shawn, Martha Graham, and Merce Cunningham.	H B	9–12	H–SS	HCC
Medearis, Angela Shelf. *Dancing with the Indians.* New York: Holiday House, 1991. While attending a Seminole Indian celebration, an African-American family watches and then joins in several exciting dances.	WC	4–5	H–SS	AP HCC
Miller, Luree. *The Black Hat Dances: Two Buddhist Boys in the Himalayas.* New York: Dodd, Mead, 1987. This book describes the influence of Buddhist beliefs on the lives of two boys, one learning to be a farmer, the other studying to be a monk. Their preparations for and participation in the Black Hat Dances, whose purpose is to drive out evil, make a fitting culmination to this look at Buddhism.	WC	6–8	H–SS	HCC
Morris, Ann. *Dancing to America.* New York: Dutton, 1994. Anton loves to dance. As a small child in Russia, he dreamed of being a ballet dancer and began training there. As his dreams become a reality, he still dances, but in a new country. This is a portrait of a young male dancer and his commitment to his art.	B	6–8		HCC

Focus: B—Biography and autobiography; **C**—Collection of works; **H**—History; **S**—Story; **T**—Techniques or skills; **WC**—World cultures
Related discipline: D—Dance; **E–LA**—English–language arts; **H–SS**—History–social science; **MA**—Mathematics; **MU**—Music; **S**—Science; **TH**—Theatre; **VA**—Visual arts
Framework **component: AP**—Artistic perception; **AV**—Aesthetic valuing; **CE**—Creative expression; **HCC**—Historical and cultural context

✪ Denotes film or videotape

	Focus	Grade level	Related discipline	Framework component

Morris, Ann. *On Their Toes: A Russian Ballet School.* New York: Atheneum, 1991.

| H | 4–5 | H–SS | HCC |

The author introduces us to the students of the Vaganora Choreographic Institute. Photographs by Ken Hayman offer glimpses of activities behind the scenes and of rehearsals. This book will serve as an inspiration for any young dancer.

Nagrin, Daniel. *Dance and the Specific Image: Improvisation.* Pittsburgh, Penn.: University of Pittsburgh Press, 1994.

| T | 9–12 | | AP CE |

A legendary performer, choreographer, and teacher, Nagrin explores the roots of his aesthetic philosophy. Over 100 improvisational structures created with his company, the Workgroup, are included.

O'Connor, Barbara. *Barefoot Dancer: The Story of Isadora Duncan.* Minneapolis, Minn.: Carolrhoda, 1994.

| B | 6–8 | D H–SS | HCC |

The author describes the life, joys, and tragedies of the modern dancer who created a spontaneous, free-form dance style which was often accompanied by literary readings and nondance music.

Padgette, Paul. *The Dance Photography of Carl Van Vechten.* New York: Schirmer, 1981.

| H | 6–8 | H–SS | HCC |

Carl Van Vechten was the first journalist to write about dance in the daily newspapers in America. Photographs and the text reflect the history of dance through his lens.

Patrick, Denise Lewis. *Red Dancing Shoes.* New York: Tambourine, 1993.

| S | K–3 | E–LA | AP |

A young girl receives a pair of red dancing shoes from her grandmama, inspiring her to dance through town and show them off to everyone she knows. Enhanced by the paintings of James E. Ransome, the story shows that respect for family and traditions can be a motivation to learning.

Pinkney, Andrea Davis. *Alvin Ailey.* New York: Hyperion, 1993.

| B | 6–8 | VA | HCC |

The life, dancing, and choreography of Alvin Ailey, who created his own modern dance company to explore the African-American experience, are the subjects of this colorful book. The bold scratch board and pastel illustrations by Brian Pinkney fortify the narrative.

Focus: B—Biography and autobiography; **C**—Collection of works; **H**—History; **S**—Story; **T**—Techniques or skills; **WC**—World cultures
Related discipline: D—Dance; **E–LA**—English-language arts; **H–SS**—History–social science; **MA**—Mathematics; **MU**—Music; **S**—Science; **TH**—Theatre; **VA**—Visual arts
Framework component: **AP**—Artistic perception; **AV**—Aesthetic valuing; **CE**—Creative expression; **HCC**—Historical and cultural context
✪ Denotes film or videotape

	Focus	Grade level	Related discipline	Framework component
Price, C. *Dance on the Dusty Earth*. New York: Scribner's, 1979.	WC	6–8		HCC AV
Author Price captures the feel of traditional dances in this appealing book. Through drawings, the author looks at the dances of native peoples throughout the world. One fascinating feature is the discussion of how hands have been used by different cultures to tell stories through dance.				
Roalf, Peggy. *Looking at Paintings—Dancers*. New York: Hyperion, 1992.	H	4–5	VA	HCC
Selected paintings capture dance through the eyes of visual artists, whose biographies are also included.				
Rosenberg, Jane. *Dance Me a Story: Twelve Tales from the Classic Ballets*. New York: Thames and Hudson, 1985.	S	6–8	MU	HCC AV
Rosenberg retells 12 great ballets as fairy tales set to music and told through the medium of dance. The author has recreated as fully as possible, in words and pictures, the actual experience of a ballet performance.				
Schick, Eleanor. *I Have Another Language—The Language Is Dance*. New York, Macmillan, 1992.	S	K–3	E–LA	AP
When a young girl dances, she discovers she can express the thoughts and feelings which she could not put into words.				
Schroeder, Alan. *Ragtime Tumpie*. Boston: Little, Brown, 1989.	S	6–8	E–LA H–SS	AP HCC
This fictional account of the childhood of the entertainer Josephine Baker tells of a young black girl who longs to find the opportunity to dance amid the poverty and vivacious street life of St. Louis in the early 1900s. The illustrations are by Bernie Fuchs.				
Shannon, George. *Dancing in the Breeze*. New York: Bradbury, 1991.	S	K–3		AP
A lilting verse by poet and storyteller George Shannon echoes the movements of the evening breeze as it leads papa and baby in a dance through a garden filled with flowers. Their playful good spirits and moments of grace are captured in Jacqueline Roger's animated watercolor scenes.				
Simon, Carly. *Amy the Dancing Bear*. New York: Doubleday, 1989.	S	K–3	E–LA	AP
This is a simple, affecting story of Amy, a bear who dances the night away, and her mother, who wishes she would go to bed. In a satisfying twist, her mother falls asleep while waiting for the dancing to stop—and Amy puts her to bed.				

Focus: **B**—Biography and autobiography; **C**—Collection of works; **H**—History; **S**—Story; **T**—Techniques or skills; **WC**—World cultures
Related discipline: **D**—Dance; **E–LA**—English–language arts; **H–SS**—History–social science; **MA**—Mathematics; **MU**—Music; **S**—Science; **TH**—Theatre; **VA**—Visual arts
Framework **component:** **AP**—Artistic perception; **AV**—Aesthetic valuing; **CE**—Creative expression; **HCC**—Historical and cultural context

✪ Denotes film or videotape

	Focus	Grade level	Related discipline	Framework component
Smith, Lucy. *Dance.* San Francisco: Dale Rettinger, 1986.	H B	9–12	E–LA H–SS	AP HCC

A companion book to *Ballet,* by Annabel Thomas, *Dance* includes sections on tap dance, jazz dance, theatre, Merce Cunningham, and Martha Graham. Excellent pictures are integrated with the comprehensive, realistic text.

	Focus	Grade level	Related discipline	Framework component
Spinelli, Eileen. *Boy, Can He Dance!* New York: Four Winds, 1993.	S	4–5		AV

Tony's father is a hotel chef who expects Tony to become a chef, too: He has no sympathy with his son's greatest interest—dancing—which Tony has done since before he could walk. The illustrations by Paul Yalowitz are sophisticated yet accessible.

	Focus	Grade level	Related discipline	Framework component
Stapler, Sarah. *Cordelia, Dance!* New York: Dial, 1990.	S	K–3	E–LA	AP

Cordelia's dream has come true—she is going to dance class. Her clumsiness is a disappointment until she finds a kindred spirit. Students will like the watercolor paintings which complement the text.

	Focus	Grade level	Related discipline	Framework component
Taylor, Paul. *Private Domain.* San Francisco: North Point, 1988.	B	9–12		HCC

In this autobiography, nominated for a National Book Critics Circle Award in 1987, Paul Taylor discusses his early work with Martha Graham and Merce Cunningham, the early years of his own dance company, his world tours, and his progression as a choreographer.

	Focus	Grade level	Related discipline	Framework component
Tharp, Twyla. *Push Comes to Shove.* New York: Bantam, 1993.	B	9–12		HCC

This is a provocative self-portrait of a woman coming to terms with herself as a major artist.

	Focus	Grade level	Related discipline	Framework component
Thomas, Annabel. *Ballet.* San Francisco: Dale Rettinger, 1986.	H T	4–5		AP HCC

An essential ballet vocabulary is explained in clear prose and attractive, helpful illustrations. The section on famous dancers and choreographers is very thorough and helps students understand their background and influences.

	Focus	Grade level	Related discipline	Framework component
Thomas, Tony. *That's Dancing!* New York: Harry Abrams, 1994.	H	9–12	VA	HCC

This book focuses on dance in Hollywood films and on the lives and work of ten outstanding dancers.

Focus: B—Biography and autobiography; **C**—Collection of works; **H**—History; **S**—Story; **T**—Techniques or skills; **WC**—World cultures

Related discipline: D—Dance; **E–LA**—English–language arts; **H–SS**—History–social science; **MA**—Mathematics; **MU**—Music; **S**—Science; **TH**—Theatre; **VA**—Visual arts

Framework **component: AP**—Artistic perception; **AV**—Aesthetic valuing; **CE**—Creative expression; **HCC**—Historical and cultural context

✪ Denotes film or videotape

	Focus	Grade level	Related discipline	Framework component
Tracey, Hugh. *African Dances of the Witwatersrand Gold Mines.* Johannesburg, South Africa: Cape Times Ltd., Parow, C.P., 1952.	WC	9–12	H–SS	HCC
Waddell, Martin. *Little Mo.* Cambridge, Mass.: Candlewick Press, 1993.	S	K–3	E–LA	AP
Walsh, Ellen. *Hop Jump.* New York: Harcourt Brace, 1993.	S	K–3	VA	AV

Tracey, Hugh. *African Dances of the Witwatersrand Gold Mines.* Johannesburg, South Africa: Cape Times Ltd., Parow, C.P., 1952.

This classic book highlights the dances of the various African cultural groups who work in the gold mines. Although the African country dances have been transported into the environment of modern industry and undergone a corresponding mutation, they still have the essence of the originals.

Waddell, Martin. *Little Mo.* Cambridge, Mass.: Candlewick Press, 1993.

When Little Mo ventures onto the slippery ice, she finds out that sliding isn't as easy as it looks. When the Big Ones come to help, she discovers she likes to slide and glide with them. Watercolor illustrations by Jill Barton enhance the text.

Walsh, Ellen. *Hop Jump.* New York: Harcourt Brace, 1993.

Betsy is bored by hopping and jumping like all the other frogs. Looking for a way to express herself, Betsy tries imitating falling leaves and soon discovers dancing. This is a gentle lesson in diversity and tolerance, beautifully enhanced by colorful collages.

Focus: B—Biography and autobiography; **C**—Collection of works; **H**—History; **S**—Story; **T**—Techniques or skills; **WC**—World cultures
Related discipline: D—Dance; **E–LA**—English–language arts; **H–SS**—History–social science; **MA**—Mathematics; **MU**—Music; **S**—Science; **TH**—Theatre; **VA**—Visual arts
Framework **component: AP**—Artistic perception; **AV**—Aesthetic valuing; **CE**—Creative expression; **HCC**—Historical and cultural context

✪ Denotes film or videotape

Music

	Focus	Grade level	Related discipline	Framework component
Bailey, Bernadine. *Bells, Bells, Bells*. New York: Dodd, Mead, 1978.	H	6–8	H–SS	HCC
Beginning with Chinese examples in 4000 B.C., this history of bells includes casting, tuning, hand-bell ringing, and carillon playing. Stories of famous bells, such as Big Ben and the Liberty Bell, are generously illustrated with photographs.				
Barnes, Joyce A. *The Baby Grand, The Moon in July, and Me*. New York: Penguin, 1994.	S	6–8	E–LA	AP
In 1969 the launching of the *Apollo II* moon rocket fuels ten-year-old Annie's dream of becoming an astronaut. Annie's brother dreams of becoming a jazz musician and buys a piano on credit. She realizes that it will take hard work to overcome family problems.				
Barrett, Mary Brigid. *Sing to the Stars*. Boston: Little, Brown, 1994.	S	K–3	VA	AP AV
Ephram helps his blind friend, Mr. Washington, remember the rhythms and regain his ability to play the piano he hasn't touched since he lost his sight. This poignant story is illustrated with brilliant pastel drawings by Sandra Speidel.				
Beirue, Barbara. *A Pianist's Debut: Preparing for the Concert Stage*. Minneapolis, Minn.: Carolrhoda, 1990.	S	6–8		AP
An eleven-year-old piano student describes her early interest in music, her first piano competition, her experience of traveling with her grandmother from Los Angeles to New York to attend the Julliard School of Music, and her aspiration to become a concert pianist.				
Berger, Gilda. *USA for Africa: Rock Aid in the Eighties*. New York: Franklin Watts, 1987.	H	6–8		HCC
Fund-raising concerts and records produced by popular musicians to benefit charities, including projects such as Band Aid, Live Aid, and Farm Aid, are discussed. Photographs illustrate the events.				
Berger, Melvin. *The Story of Folk Music*. New York: Phillips, 1976.	H B	6–8	H–SS	HCC
Berger discusses how and why American folk music evolved and presents biographical information on singers from Woody Guthrie to John Denver. Also see *Folk Music in America*, by Brian Van Der Horst.				
Blackwood, Alan. *The Orchestra: An Introduction to the World of Classical Music*. Brookfield, Conn.: Millbrook, 1993.	H	6–8	H–SS	HCC
This book traces the history of the orchestra and discusses the musical instruments that make up the orchestral families.				

Focus: B—Biography and autobiography; **C**—Collection of works; **H**—History; **S**—Story; **T**—Techniques or skills; **WC**—World cultures
Related discipline: D—Dance; **E–LA**—English–language arts; **H–SS**—History–social science; **MA**—Mathematics; **MU**—Music; **S**—Science; **TH**—Theatre; **VA**—Visual arts
Framework **component: AP**—Artistic perception; **AV**—Aesthetic valuing; **CE**—Creative expression; **HCC**—Historical and cultural context

○ Denotes film or videotape

	Focus	Grade level	Related discipline	Framework component
Broven, John. *South to Louisiana: The Music of the Cajun Bayous*. New York: Pelican, 1987.	H	9–12	H–SS	HCC
From Cajun country music to the Cajun revival, the author chronicles the development and range of Cajun music. Also included is an appendix with a time chart, a list of Cajun recordings, and other references.				
Burningham, John. *Trubloff: The Mouse Who Wanted to Play the Balalaika*. New York: Crown, 1992.	S	K–3	VA	AP AV
Trubloff, of the Trub family, runs away with Gypsies to learn to play the balalaika and returns home just in time to save his family. The bold illustrations by Burningham complement the story.				
Cash, Johnny. *Man in Black*. Grand Rapids, Mich.: Zondervan Publishing House, 1976.	B	9–12	H–SS	HCC
This is Cash's story of his rise to fame, his failures, his period of drug addiction, and the revival of his faith and fortune. This book provides insight into the pressures and problems inherent in show business.				
Clement, Claude. *Musician from the Darkness*. New York: Little, Brown, 1989.	S	K–3	E–LA	AP
A young member of a tribe discovers the effects of music on his environment and well-being in this beautifully written book, illustrated by John Howe.				
Closson, Ernest. *History of the Piano*. Edited by Robin Gordina. New York: St. Martin's, 1982.	H	9–12	H–SS	HCC
From ancient hand percussion to the keyboards invented in the fourteenth century, this book provides a unique history of the piano. It includes profiles of pianists such as Claudio Arrau, Vladimir Ashkenazy, and André Watts.				
Collier, James Lincoln. *Duke Ellington*. New York: Macmillan, 1991.	B	4–5	H–SS	HCC
A noted jazz critic and musician, James Lincoln Collier details the life of musician and composer Duke Ellington.				
Cornell, Jean Gay. *Louis Armstrong: Ambassador Satchmo.* New York: Garrard, 1972.	B	4–5	H–SS	HCC
The exuberance of Satchmo's trumpet playing and the vitality of his contribution to jazz are conveyed in this biography.				
Cutler, Ivor. *Doris*. New York: Tambourine, 1992.	S	K–3	E–LA	AP
Doris the hen and Oliver Parrot discover that their duets are not only fun to sing but also lucrative.				

Focus: **B**—Biography and autobiography; **C**—Collection of works; **H**—History; **S**—Story; **T**—Techniques or skills; **WC**—World cultures

Related discipline: **D**—Dance; **E–LA**—English-language arts; **H–SS**—History-social science; **MA**—Mathematics; **MU**—Music; **S**—Science; **TH**—Theatre; **VA**—Visual arts

Framework **component:** **AP**—Artistic perception; **AV**—Aesthetic valuing; **CE**—Creative expression; **HCC**—Historical and cultural context

○ Denotes film or videotape

	Focus	Grade level	Related discipline	Framework component
Driscoll, Debbie. *Jenny Come Along*. New York: Doubleday, 1995.	S	K–3	E–LA	AP
The simple, lyrical verses based on a traditional American folk song follow a little girl through a day filled with familiar pleasures.				
Englander, Roger. *Opera: What's All the Screaming About?* New York: Walker, 1983.	H	6–8	H–SS	HCC
This is an insightful introduction to opera in all its dimensions.				
Ewen, David A. *Great Men of American Popular Song*. Englewood Cliffs, N.J.: Prentice-Hall, 1972.	H B	9–12	H–SS	HCC
Ewen's biographies, personal portraits, and critical evaluations of major contributors provide an interesting history of the popular song from colonial times to 1970.				
Feather, Leonard. *From Satchmo to Miles*. Briarcliff Manor, N.Y.: Stein and Day, 1974.	H B	9–12	H–SS	HCC
This book includes portraits of jazz greats such as Duke Ellington, Ella Fitzgerald, Count Basie, the Bird, Ray Charles, Don Ellis, and Miles Davis. It also traces the history of major developments in jazz.				
Ferris, Jeri. *What I Had Was Singing: The Story of Marian Anderson*. Minneapolis, Minn.: Carolrhoda, 1990.	B	6–8	H–SS	HCC
The life of Marian Anderson, from her childhood in Philadelphia through her work as a United States delegate to the United Nations, is the subject of this biography.				
Ferry, Charles. *One More Time!* New York: Houghton Mifflin, 1985.	S	6–8	H–SS	AP HCC
This story of a young band on tour as World War II comes to a close reflects the general euphoria of a young and "swinging" America.				
Fleischman, Paul. *Rondo in C*. New York: Harper, 1988.	S	4–5	E–LA	AP
In this story of a child's piano recital, each audience member's thoughts are graphically revealed in the illustrations of Janet Wentworth.				
Floyd, Samuel A. *Black Music in the Harlem Renaissance: A Collection of Essays*. Westport, Conn.: Greenwood, 1993.	H	9–12	H–SS	HCC
The author examines African-American music during the Harlem Renaissance, a movement in the 1920s that pressed for economic, social, and cultural equality. A rich bibliography of music composed during this era is included.				

Focus: B—Biography and autobiography; **C**—Collection of works; **H**—History; **S**—Story; **T**—Techniques or skills; **WC**—World cultures
Related discipline: D—Dance; **E–LA**—English–language arts; **H–SS**—History–social science; **MA**—Mathematics; **MU**—Music; **S**—Science;
  TH—Theatre; **VA**—Visual arts
Framework **component: AP**—Artistic perception; **AV**—Aesthetic valuing; **CE**—Creative expression; **HCC**—Historical and cultural context

🔾 Denotes film or videotape

	Focus	Grade level	Related discipline	Framework component
Ford, M. Thomas. *Paula Abdul: Straight Up.* New York: Dillon, 1992.	B	6–8	H–SS D	HCC
The life of the entertainer whose energetic choreography changed the look of cheerleading and rock videos and led to her multifaceted career is described in this biography.				
Foster, Karen. *Rattles, Bells, and Chiming Bars.* Brookfield, Conn.: Millbrook, 1992.	H	4–5	H–SS	HCC
Focusing on the principle of rhythm, the author presents a wide range of percussion instruments, from Spanish castanets to the xylophone. The author covers the production and use of these instruments in different cultures.				
Gonzalez, Fernando. *Gloria Estefan.* Brookfield, Conn.: Millbrook, 1993.	B	6–8		HCC
The life of the popular Hispanic-American singer Gloria Estefan is traced from her childhood in Cuba, through her performances with the Miami Sound Machine, to her current acclaim.				
Goodman, Joan E. *Songs from Home.* San Diego: Harcourt Brace, 1994.	B	4–5	H–SS	HCC
In Rome in 1969, after years of being adrift in Europe, eleven-year-old Anna and her father sing in the streets for money. But Anna dreams of having a normal home and family life.				
Greenfield, Eloise. *Paul Robeson.* New York: Crowell, 1975.	B	4–5	H–SS	HCC
Reflecting the dynamic spirit of Robeson's life and accomplishments, this book describes his struggle and fight for freedom.				
Guthrie, Woody, with Marjorie Mazia. *Woody's Twenty Grow-Big Songs.* New York: HarperCollins, 1992.	C	4–5	H–SS	AP HCC
This reprint of a 1940s songbook published by Woody Guthrie contains an illustrated collection of songs, a bit of their history, and their musical arrangements.				
Haskins, James. *Black Music in America: A History Through Its People.* New York: Crowell, 1987.	H	9–12	H–SS	HCC
This book covers the totality of black contributions to music in America from early slave music to the rhythms, blues, and arias of the 1950s and the new directions of the 1970s and 1980s.				
Hautzig, David. *DJ's Ratings and Hook Tapes: Pop Music Broadcasting.* New York: Macmillan, 1993.	H B	6–8		AP HCC
The work of a program director, researchers, disk jockeys, and other key figures are described in a behind-the-scenes look at a radio station.				

Focus: **B**—Biography and autobiography; **C**—Collection of works; **H**—History; **S**—Story; **T**—Techniques or skills; **WC**—World cultures
Related discipline: **D**—Dance; **E–LA**—English–language arts; **H–SS**—History–social science; **MA**—Mathematics; **MU**—Music; **S**—Science; **TH**—Theatre; **VA**—Visual arts
Framework component: **AP**—Artistic perception; **AV**—Aesthetic valuing; **CE**—Creative expression; **HCC**—Historical and cultural context

◎ Denotes film or videotape

	Focus	Grade level	Related discipline	Framework component
Hru, Dakari. *Joshua's Masai Mask.* New York: Lee and Low, 1993.	S	6–8	H–SS VA	HCC AV
Fearing that his classmates will ridicule his playing the kalimba in the school talent show, Joshua uses a magical Masai mask to transform himself into different people. He believes these disguises will make him more interesting, until he realizes that his own identity is valuable.				
Hughes, Langston. *The First Book of Jazz.* New York: Franklin Watts, 1976.	H	6–8	H–SS	HCC
Hughes traces the history of jazz from its African origins to the modern forms built around the career of Louis Armstrong. Cliff Roberts is the illustrator.				
Hurd, Michael. *The Orchestra.* New York: Facts on File, 1980.	H	6–8	H–SS	AP HCC
Hurd discusses the evolution of the orchestra, great conductors, the history and structure of instruments, and particular orchestras. Biographies of 101 conductors are included.				
An Illustrated Songbook for Young People. New York: Metropolitan Museum of Art, 1987.	C	6–8	H–SS	HCC AV
This is an illustrated collection of 61 traditional songs. The illustrations are reproductions of paintings and other works of art from the Metropolitan Museum of Art's collection. For instance, *The Teton Range,* by Thomas Moran, illustrates "America the Beautiful."				
Johnston, Tony. *Grandpa's Song.* New York: Dial, 1991.	S	4–5	VA H–SS	AP HCC
This is a story about a young girl's beloved, exuberant, yet forgetful grandfather. She helps him by singing their favorite song. The luminous watercolor illustrations by Bradley Sneed help tell a story about the transmission of family traditions and values.				
Jones, Hettie. *Big Star Fallin' Mama.* New York: Viking, 1995.	H B	6–8		HCC
With grace and style, the author explores the lives and times of Ma Rainey, Bessie Smith, Mahalia Jackson, Billie Holiday, and Aretha Franklin. Each of these gifted singers has made a unique contribution to the blues and to the world.				
Jones, K. Maurice. *Say It Loud! The Story of Rap Music.* Brookfield, Conn.: Millbrook, 1994.	H	9–12	TH	HCC AV
This history of rap music identifies its roots in slave music and communication. Many photographs enhance chapters on technology, free speech, global issues, and style.				

Focus: B—Biography and autobiography; **C**—Collection of works; **H**—History; **S**—Story; **T**—Techniques or skills; **WC**—World cultures
Related discipline: D—Dance; **E–LA**—English–language arts; **H–SS**—History–social science; **MA**—Mathematics; **MU**—Music; **S**—Science; **TH**—Theatre; **VA**—Visual arts
Framework **component: AP**—Artistic perception; **AV**—Aesthetic valuing; **CE**—Creative expression; **HCC**—Historical and cultural context
✪ Denotes film or videotape

	Focus	Grade level	Related discipline	Framework component
Kaufman, Fredrick, and John P. Guckin. *The African Roots of Jazz.* Sherman Oaks, Calif.: Alfred Publishing, 1979.	H	9–12	H–SS	HCC
The authors explore the musical and cultural roots of jazz. Witchcraft, musical characteristics, instruments, and African music today are also discussed.				
Komaiko, Leah. *I Like the Music.* New York: HarperCollins, 1987.	S	4–5		AP
A little girl who loves street music learns to love the symphony as well when her grandmother takes her to an outdoor concert.				
Kraus, Robert. *Musical Max. New York: Simon* and Schuster, 1990.	S	K–3	E–LA	AP HCC
Many instruments are featured in this book, since the talented Max wants to play every instrument. Pictures by Jose Aruego and Ariane Dewey help tell Max's story.				
Krementz, Jill. *A Very Young Musician.* New York: Simon and Schuster, 1991.	S	4–5		HCC AV
Ten-year-old Josh learns how to play the trumpet by taking lessons and attending performances of musicians like Billy Taylor and Wynton Marsalis.				
Krohn. *Elvis Presley, the King.* Minneapolis, Minn.: Learner, 1994.	B	4–5	E–LA	HCC
This book examines the childhood, musical career, films, family life, and legacy of rock star Elvis Presley.				
Krull Kathleen. *Alex Fitzgerald, TV Star.* New York: Little, Brown, 1991.	S	4–5		AP
A pianist has an opportunity to perform on television. This is a story of a young girl on the road to fame and the lessons she learns on that journey.				
Krull, Kathleen. *Gonna Sing My Head Off! American Folk Songs.* New York: Knopf, 1992.	C	4–5	H–SS	CE
The author offers a history of each song in this diverse collection of American folk songs. Rich in tradition and American values, this is an appropriate gift for any child.				
Krull, Kathleen. *Lives of the Musicians: Good Times, Bad Times (And What the Neighbors Thought).* San Diego: Harcourt Brace, 1993.	B	6–8	E–LA	HCC
The lives of 20 composers and musicians, ranging from Vivaldi, Mozart, and Bach to Gershwin, Gilbert and Sullivan, and Woody Guthrie, are profiled in this eclectic, humorous, and informative collection.				

Focus: B—Biography and autobiography; **C**—Collection of works; **H**—History; **S**—Story; **T**—Techniques or skills; **WC**—World cultures

Related discipline: D—Dance; **E–LA**—English–language arts; **H–SS**—History–social science; **MA**—Mathematics; **MU**—Music; **S**—Science; **TH**—Theatre; **VA**—Visual arts

Framework **component: AP**—Artistic perception; **AV**—Aesthetic valuing; **CE**—Creative expression; **HCC**—Historical and cultural context

○ Denotes film or videotape

	Focus	Grade level	Related discipline	Framework component
Kuskin, Karla. *The Philharmonic Gets Dressed.* New York: HarperCollins, 1982. The 105 members of the philharmonic orchestra get ready for a performance. In a charming progression, the members begin with showers or baths and end up coming together to make beautiful music.	S	6–8		AP HCC
Landon, H. C. Robbins. *1791: Mozart's Last Year.* New York: Macmillan, 1990. This book describes Mozart's life in the Austrian court, his last musical works, his illness, and his relationships.	H B	9–12	H–SS	HCC
Laufe, Abe. *Broadway's Greatest Musicals: The New Illustrated Edition* (Third edition). New York: Funk and Wagnalls, 1977. This valuable resource contains summaries of plots, production anecdotes, descriptions, reviews, and the financial status for Broadway musicals of different eras. Chapters focus on the early years—1884–1927, on the Depression years, and on major shows.	H	6–8	H–SS	HCC
Lemieux, Michele. *Peter and the Wolf.* New York: Morrow Junior Books, 1991. Sergei Prokofiev's *Peter and the Wolf* is brought to life through literature and vivid paintings.	S	K–3	H–SS VA	HCC
Levinson, Nancy Suriler. *Sweet Notes, Sour Notes.* New York: Lodestar, 1993. David, growing up in the 1920s, discovers that perseverance is the only way to succeed in learning to play the violin.	S	6–8	E–LA	AP AV
"Louis Armstrong and the Art of Jazz," *Cobblestone: The History Magazine for Young People.* Peterborough, N.H.: Cobblestone Publishing, October, 1994. This entire issue of *Cobblestone* is devoted to the internationally known jazz musician Louis Armstrong. Articles detail his growing up with jazz in New Orleans, his international adventures, and the artworks he made in his leisure time.	B	4–5		HCC
Lyttelton, Humphrey. *The Best of Jazz II.* New York: Taplinger, 1981. This is a readable and musically sophisticated account of the greats of the Swing Era and their world from 1931 to 1944.	H B	6–8	H–SS	HCC
McKissack, Fredrick, and Patricia McKissack. *Marian Anderson: A Great Singer.* Hillside, N.J.: Enslow, 1991. This is the biography of the African-American singer who struggled against prejudice to become one of the great opera performers of the century.	B	K–3	H–SS	HCC

Focus: B—Biography and autobiography; **C**—Collection of works; **H**—History; **S**—Story; **T**—Techniques or skills; **WC**—World cultures
Related discipline: D—Dance; **E–LA**—English–language arts; **H–SS**—History–social science; **MA**—Mathematics; **MU**—Music; **S**—Science;
  TH—Theatre; **VA**—Visual arts
Framework **component: AP**—Artistic perception; **AV**—Aesthetic valuing; **CE**—Creative expression; **HCC**—Historical and cultural context

◎ Denotes film or videotape

	Focus	Grade level	Related discipline	Framework component
McLerran, Alice. *Dream Song.* New York: Tambourine Books, 1992.	S	4–5	E–LA	AP
Vivid illustrations help tell the story of Pavel, who searches fields, forests, and mountains for the song he hears each night in his dream, unaware that the true source is in his own home.				
Mathis, Sharon Bell. *Ray Charles.* New York: Crowell, 1973.	B	4–5		HCC
This is a clearly written biography of the world-famous blues, gospel, and jazz entertainer.				
Medearis, Angela Shelf. Little Louis and the *Jazz Band: The Story of Louis "Satchmo" Armstrong.* New York: Lodestar, 1994.	B	4–5	H–SS	HCC
This book focuses on the childhood of Louis Armstrong and his entrance into the world of the jazz band in New Orleans. Drawings by Anna Rich illustrate the early years, and photographs help tell the story as Armstrong becomes famous.				
Meyer, Carolyn M. *Rock Band—Big Men in a Great Big Town.* New York: Atheneum, A Margaret McElderry Book, 1980.	B	9–12	H–SS	HCC
An accounting of the role of organization, training, and luck in the efforts of a fictional rock band to make "the big time." Meyer provides a perceptive examination of the background, skills, demands, personal relationships, and good luck which constitute a career in rock and roll.				
Mitchell, Barbara. *America, I Hear You.* Minneapolis, Minn.: Carolrhoda, 1988.	B	9–12	H–SS	HCC
This is a biography of George Gershwin. The same publisher and author have produced biographies of Scott Joplin (*Raggin'*) and Beatrix Potter. (*The Country Artist*).				
Monceaux, Morgan. *Jazz: My Music, My People.* New York: Knopf, 1994.	H B	4–5	H–SS	HCC
Short biographies accompanied by vibrant portraits by Monceaux of each jazz musician make up this readable history of jazz. This book could be also used in a visual arts class as a model for expressive use of line and color.				
Morris, Ann. *Dancing to America.* New York: Dutton, 1994.	B	6–8		HCC
Anton loves to dance. As a small child in Russia, he dreamed of being a ballet dancer and began training there. As his dream becomes a reality, he still dances, but in a new country. With photographs by Paul Koluik, this portrait of a young male dancer with the School of American Ballet in New York City chronicles his growth as a dancer and commitment to his art.				

Focus: B—Biography and autobiography; **C**—Collection of works; **H**—History; **S**—Story; **T**—Techniques or skills; **WC**—World cultures
Related discipline: D—Dance; **E–LA**—English–language arts; **H–SS**—History–social science; **MA**—Mathematics; **MU**—Music; **S**—Science; **TH**—Theatre; **VA**—Visual arts
Framework **component: AP**—Artistic perception; **AV**—Aesthetic valuing; **CE**—Creative expression; **HCC**—Historical and cultural context

○ Denotes film or videotape

	Focus	Grade level	Related discipline	Framework component
✪ *The Nature of Music.* RM Arts, n.d. Order from HomeVision, 5547 N. Ravenswood Avenue, Chicago, IL 60640-1199, (800) 826-3456. People incorporate music into sacred rituals and use it for healing, dancing, worship, and protest. These three programs on one videotape explore the importance of music in societies around the world.	H	9–12		HCC
O'Donnell, Elizabeth Lee. *Sing Me a Window.* New York: Morrow Junior Books, 1993. A child requests a bedtime song about her teddy bear and their adventures together. The story is told in verse, and the watercolor illustrations by Melissa Sweet enhance the telling.	S	4–5	VA	AP
Otsuka, Yuzo. *Suho and the White Horse.* New York: Viking, 1981. A touching retelling of an ancient Mongolian folktale conveys how music helps us to ennoble our grief.	WC	4–5	H–SS	HCC
Paker, Josephine. *Breathing the Drum.* Brookfield, Conn.: Millbrook, 1992. This book effectively explores the nature of sound through drums, from Latin America to India, from Africa to Japan. The history of drums in each culture is presented and illustrated with numerous photographs, drawings, and reproductions of paintings.	WC	6–8	H–SS S MA	AP HCC
Paker, Josephine. *Music from Strings.* Brookfield, Conn.: Millbrook, 1992. Rich with illustrations and photographs, this book covers the wide range of string instruments, their place in different cultures, and the musical principles behind their use and production.	H	4–5	H–SS S MA	AP HCC
Panassie, Hugues. *Louis Armstrong.* New York: Da Capo Press, 1980. This personal portrait is also a critical examination of Armstrong's music by a French jazz critic who was a close friend of Armstrong.	B	6–8	H–SS	HCC
Patterson, Charles. *Marian Anderson.* New York: Franklin Watts, 1988. Historian Patterson chronicles the life of Marian Anderson as a singer and an African American.	B	6–8	H–SS	HCC

Focus: B—Biography and autobiography; **C**—Collection of works; **H**—History; **S**—Story; **T**—Techniques or skills; **WC**—World cultures
Related discipline: D—Dance; **E–LA**—English-language arts; **H–SS**—History-social science; **MA**—Mathematics; **MU**—Music; **S**—Science; **TH**—Theatre; **VA**—Visual arts
Framework **component: AP**—Artistic perception; **AV**—Aesthetic valuing; **CE**—Creative expression; **HCC**—Historical and cultural context
✪ Denotes film or videotape

	Focus	Grade level	Related discipline	Framework component

Peterson, Jeanne Whitehouse. *My Mama Sings.* New York: HarperCollins, 1994.

| | S | 4–5 | VA | AP |

This is the story of a little boy and his mama, who had special old songs for all occasions. When the time comes that she has no song ready, her little boy supplies one. The luminous illustrations by Sandra Speidel provide a richness to the rhythm of the prose.

Pillar, Marjorie. *Join the Band.* New York: HarperCollins, 1992.

| | S | K–3 | E–LA | AP |

A young flutist narrates this picture book about a school band, its range of instruments, its practice sessions, and, finally, its concert performance. It is illustrated with color photographs.

Politi, Leo. *Mr. Fong's Toy Shop.* New York: Scribner's, 1978.

| | S | 4–5 | E–LA | AP HCC |

Music is a part of the lovely Moon Festival celebration.

Pollock, Bruce. *In Their Own Words: Lyrics and Lyricists, 1965–74.* New York: Macmillan/Collier, 1975.

| | H B | 6–8 | E–LA | HCC |

Twenty successful lyricists (or lyricist-composers) tell how they write their songs. The writers include Hal David, Buffy St. Marie, Harry Chapin, Frank Zappa, and Peter Townsend.

Raffi. *Like Me and You.* New York: Crown, 1994.

| | S | K–3 | E–LA | AP |

This is an illustrated version of Raffi's song about children all over the world who are much like one another, despite the fact that they live in different countries. Lillian Hoban's illustrations enhance the text.

Raschka, Chris. *Charlie Parker Played Be-Bop.* Orchard, 1992.

| | B | K–3 | H–SS | AP HCC |

Charlie Parker plays the saxophone in this vibrantly illustrated book. The rhythm of the words mimics the rhythm of jazz music.

Ray, Mary Lyn. *Pianna.* San Diego: Harcourt Brace, 1994.

| | S | 4–5 | H–SS | AP |

In a pumpkin-colored house between the railroad and Ragged Mountain lives a woman who has lived there for 80 years. If you were to visit her, she could explain all kinds of things about her life in the house when she was a girl. But the thing she would most like to do for you is play the piano. She played when she was young, and she is still playing.

Focus: B—Biography and autobiography; **C**—Collection of works; **H**—History; **S**—Story; **T**—Techniques or skills; **WC**—World cultures
Related discipline: D—Dance; **E–LA**—English–language arts; **H–SS**—History–social science; **MA**—Mathematics; **MU**—Music; **S**—Science; **TH**—Theatre; **VA**—Visual arts
Framework **component: AP**—Artistic perception; **AV**—Aesthetic valuing; **CE**—Creative expression; **HCC**—Historical and cultural context

🔾 Denotes film or videotape

	Focus	Grade level	Related discipline	Framework component
✪ *Repercussions: A Celebration of African-American Music*. RM Arts, n.d. Order from HomeVision, 5547 N. Ravenswood Avenue, Chicago, IL 60640-1199, (800) 826-3456. Seven hour-long programs celebrate America's musical legacy, forged from the Old World music of Africa and Europe. This fusion gave us the sounds of jazz, soul, blues, gospel, funk, rock, and reggae. This wide-ranging series tells the story of these musical traditions.	H	9–12	H–SS	AP HCC
Rosenberg, Jane. *Bravo! Sing Me a Story*. Introduction by Luciano Pavarotti. New York: Thames and Hudson, 1988. The lavish spectacle, the magic, the action scenery, and the music are transported from the opera stage to the printed page.	S	6–8	E–LA	HCC
Rowley, Kay. *Rockworld: Concerts*. New York: Crestwood House, 1991. This brief history of rock and roll covers the staging and production of concerts of rock stars from the Beatles to Prince. A glossary is included.	H	4–5	H–SS	AP HCC
Rowley, Kay. *Rockworld: Music*. New York: Crestwood House, 1992. The origins of popular music and the various genres which have developed over the last 50 years, ranging from rock and roll to progressive and reggae, are described in this book.	H	4–5	H–SS	AP HCC
Rowley, Kay. *Rockworld: Stars*. New York: Crestwood House, 1992. Following a brief history of popular music, the author portrays such legendary figures as Elvis Presley and the Beatles as they set the stage for today's rock musicians. Minibiographies of other stars and a glossary of popular music are included.	H	4–5	H–SS	HCC
Rubel, David. *Elvis Presley: The Rise of Rock and Roll*. Brookfield, Conn.: Millbrook, 1991. This biography of singer Elvis Presley tells about his life, the rise of rock music, and the social changes of the 1950s and 1960s.	B	6–8	H–SS	HCC
Salerno-Sonnenberg, Nadja. *Nadja: On My Way*. New York: Crown, 1989. This autobiographical account of the renowned violinist's rise to fame and the obstacles she encountered includes photographs of the young violinist in concert.	B	6–8	E–LA	HCC
Shankar, Ravi. *My Music, My Life*. New York: Simon and Schuster, 1968. Sitarist Ravi Shankar talks about the place of music in his life.	WC	9–12		HCC

Focus: B—Biography and autobiography; **C**—Collection of works; **H**—History; **S**—Story; **T**—Techniques or skills; **WC**—World cultures
Related discipline: D—Dance; **E–LA**—English–language arts; **H–SS**—History–social science; **MA**—Mathematics; **MU**—Music; **S**—Science; **TH**—Theatre; **VA**—Visual arts
Framework **component: AP**—Artistic perception; **AV**—Aesthetic valuing; **CE**—Creative expression; **HCC**—Historical and cultural context

✪ Denotes film or videotape

	Focus	Grade level	Related discipline	Framework component
Spence, Keith. *The Young People's Book of Music.* Brookfield, Conn.: Millbrook, 1993. This detailed work provides an encyclopedic overview of European musical traditions. The author investigates instruments, forms of music, opera, and ballet and includes brief biographies of composers.	H	9–12		AP HCC
Staines, Bill. *River.* New York: Penguin, 1994. This book is an illustration of the song "River" by Bill Staines. The expressionist paintings reflect a young person's musings on the progress of life as symbolized by the flow of the river.	S	4–5	VA	AP
Staples, Danny, and Carol Mahoney. *Flutes, Reeds, and Trumpets.* Brookfield, Conn.: Millbrook, 1992. The authors cover the development of the flute, brass instruments, and wind instruments. They discuss the creation of various types of music. Photographs and illustrations are included.	H	4–5	H–SS S MA	HCC
Staskowski, Andrea. *Movie Musicals.* New York: Learner, 1992. The author traces the development of movie musicals, including the production of such famous musicals as *West Side Story* and *Dirty Dancing*. Photographs and story lines enhance discussions of each musical.	H	4–5	D TH	HCC
Terkel, Studs. *Giants of Jazz.* New York: HarperCollins, 1975. The lives of this century's greatest jazz musicians, from Joe Oliver to Charlie Parker, are chronicled with text and photographs in this highly readable book.	H B	6–8	H–SS	HCC
Thompson, Wendy. *Composer's World* series. New York: Viking, 1993. This series comprises biographies of Beethoven, Hayden, Schubert, Debussy, Mozart, and Tchaikovsky. The biographies include discussions of the composers' works, their significance, and their place in society.	B	6–8	H–SS	HCC
Waddell, Martin. *The Happy Hedgehog Band.* Candlewick, 1992. In this book, hedgehogs make drums and create a band. The forest animals want to join in the fun by playing instruments and dancing.	S	K–3	E–LA	AP
Waldman, Neil. *America the Beautiful.* New York: Macmillan, 1993. This illustrated edition of the nineteenth-century poem, later set to music, celebrates the beauty of America. The acrylic paintings by Waldman are luminous landscapes.	C	4–5	H–SS	HCC

Focus: B—Biography and autobiography; **C**—Collection of works; **H**—History; **S**—Story; **T**—Techniques or skills; **WC**—World cultures
Related discipline: D—Dance; **E–LA**—English-language arts; **H–SS**—History-social science; **MA**—Mathematics; **MU**—Music; **S**—Science; **TH**—Theatre; **VA**—Visual arts
***Framework* component: AP**—Artistic perception; **AV**—Aesthetic valuing; **CE**—Creative expression; **HCC**—Historical and cultural context

✪ Denotes film or videotape

	Focus	Grade level	Related discipline	Framework component
Warhola, James. *The Surrey with the Fringe on Top.* New York: Simon and Schuster, 1993. This illustrated version of the Rodgers and Hammerstein song celebrates the fiftieth year of its publication. The outstanding illustrations highlight the lyrics, which feature the unusual humorous and startling juxtaposition of triple rhymes, such as *flutters, strutters,* and *shutters.*	S	4–5	E–LA	HCC
Watson, Wendy. *Fox Went Out on a Chilly Night.* New York: Lothrop, Lee and Shepard, 1994. The story of this classic folk song of a fox in pursuit of his dinner is told through Watson's vivid illustrations.	S	K–3	E–LA	AP
Weil, Lisl. *The Magic of Music.* New York: Holiday House, 1989. With text and illustrations, the author guides readers through the concepts of melody, rhythm and harmony, instruments, notation, and different types of music, from opera to rock.	H	4–5		AP AV
Weil, Lisl. *Wolferl: The First Six Years in the Life of Wolfgang Amadeus Mozart.* New York: Holiday House, 1991. Simple language and illustrations are used to describe Wolfgang Amadeus's first six years of life. A glossary of instruments and people is included.	B	K–3	H–SS	HCC
Wharton, Thomas. *Hildegard Sings.* New York: Sunburst Books, 1993. Hildegard Rhinehetter, the understudy for the lead in an opera company, has lost her voice. Can she recover in time to sing for the queen? Vivid illustrations make this an unforgettable story of a singer on the brink of stardom.	S	4–5	VA	HCC AV
Williams, Sylvia. *Leontyne Price: Opera Superstar.* Chicago: Children's Press, 1984. This is a brief biography of the African-American opera singer who is one of the most celebrated sopranos of her time and who, among other honors, opened the 1984 season of the Metropolitan Opera House in New York City.	B	4–5	H–SS	HCC
Wolfe, Rinna Evelyn. *The Calvin Simmons Story, or "Don't Call Me Maestro!"* Berkeley, Calif.: Muse Wood Press, 1994. Simmons was the first African-American conductor of a major United States orchestra. Born in San Francisco, Simmons grew up to be the conductor of the Oakland Symphony from 1978 until his death in 1982.	B	6–8	H–SS	HCC

Focus: **B**—Biography and autobiography; **C**—Collection of works; **H**—History; **S**—Story; **T**—Techniques or skills; **WC**—World cultures
Related discipline: **D**—Dance; **E–LA**—English–language arts; **H–SS**—History–social science; **MA**—Mathematics; **MU**—Music; **S**—Science; **TH**—Theatre; **VA**—Visual arts
Framework component: **AP**—Artistic perception; **AV**—Aesthetic valuing; **CE**—Creative expression; **HCC**—Historical and cultural context

✪ Denotes film or videotape

Theatre

	Focus	Grade level	Related discipline	Framework component
Aardema, Verna. *Who's in Rabbit's House?* New York: Penguin, 1979.	WC	K–3	H–SS	HCC
In this story, based on a Masai folktale, Rabbit finds an intruder in his house and, with the help of his friends, must find a way to get him out. The story is illustrated as a play presented by the African community.				
Adams, Mary Agnes. *Whoopi Goldberg: From Street to Stardom.* TAKING PART series. New York: Dillon Press, 1993.	B	6–8	H–SS	HCC
This biography of Whoopi Goldberg describes her drug-filled youth and her days as a young welfare mother that preceded her fame on Broadway. Other subjects in the TAKING PART series include Ann Bancroft, Bill Cosby, Steven Spielberg, and Paula Abdul.				
Adler, Bill. *The Letterman Wit: His Life and Humor.* New York: Carroll and Graf, 1994.	B	9–12	H–SS	HCC
Compiled from interviews with friends, colleagues, and business associates, this book is full of the brand of humor that characterizes David Letterman. See also Adler's *The Cosby Wit.*				
Aesop's Fables. Selected and illustrated by Michael Hague. New York: Henry Holt, 1985.	S	4–5	E–LA	AV
Selected fables are illustrated with beautiful paintings and engagingly interpreted.				
Aitken, Amy. *Ruby.* Scarsdale, N.Y.: Bradbury, 1979.	S	9–12	E–LA	AP
The focus of this book is on Ruby's changing dreams about what she wants to be when she grows up: rock star, author, artist, movie star, and even president.				
Alexander, Martha. *My Outrageous Friend Charlie.* New York: Dial, 1989.	S	K–3	E–LA	CE
The author transforms familiar childhood experiences into delightful stories. Children could work in groups to expand the stories and write new adventures for Charlie and Jessie on their trip around the world.				
Alexander, Sue. *Witch, Goblin, and Ghost in the Haunted Woods.* New York: Pantheon, 1981.	S	4–5	E–LA	AP
The three friends have five adventures, all of which could be expanded for creative drama.				

Focus: B—Biography and autobiography; **C**—Collection of works; **H**—History; **S**—Story; **T**—Techniques or skills; **WC**—World cultures

Related discipline: D—Dance; **E–LA**—English–language arts; **H–SS**—History–social science; **MA**—Mathematics; **MU**—Music; **S**—Science; **TH**—Theatre; **VA**—Visual arts

Framework component: **AP**—Artistic perception; **AV**—Aesthetic valuing; **CE**—Creative expression; **HCC**—Historical and cultural context

✪ Denotes film or videotape

	Focus	Grade level	Related discipline	Framework component
Aliki, Brandenberg. *The Story of Johnny Appleseed.* Englewood Cliffs, N.J.: Simon and Schuster, 1988. Lively drawings celebrate the goodness of the land and the legendary Johnny Appleseed. Also see Aliki's *My Five Senses* for a good description of the senses, with full-color illustrations.	WC	K–3	H–SS	CE
Aller, Susan Bivin. *J. M. Barrie: The Magic Behind Peter Pan.* Minneapolis, Minn.: Lerner, 1994. This biography of J. M. Barrie, the writer who never wanted to grow up, describes his antics and retells the stories which delighted the children who knew him.	B	9–12	E–LA	HCC
Anderson, Bernice G. *Trickster Tales from Prairie Lodgefires.* Nashville, Tenn.: Abingdon, 1979. This collection contains tales from the Blackfoot, Kiowa, Crow, Ponca, Dakota, and Cheyenne tribes. All of the tales could be expanded for dramatization.	WC	6–8	H–SS	AP HCC
Anderson, Joan. *Christmas on the Prairie.* New York: Ticknor and Fields (Clarion), 1985. The customs of an American Christmas were first brought to the prairies by the Dutch during the settling of the western frontier. This story was photographed at the Living History Museum at Conner Prairie Pioneer Settlement, Noblesville, Indiana.	S	4–5	H–SS	HCC
Anderson, Joy. *Juma and the Magic Jinn.* New York: Lothrop, Lee and Shepard, 1986. The exotic island of Lamu and the Muslim culture are the inspirations for this magical fairy-tale adventure.	WC	K–3	H–SS	AP
Appel, Libby. *Mask Characterization.* Carbondale: Southern Illinois University Press, 1982. This illuminating and practical guide deals with the use of masks in production and in the training of actors in body awareness, physical expressiveness, and nonverbal character development.	T	9–12	E–LA	AP HCC
Arginteanu, Judy. *The Movies of Alfred Hitchcock.* Minneapolis, Minn.: Lerner, 1994. The author analyzes the ideas and themes of the famous film director's works, including *Vertigo, Psycho,* and *The Birds.* Photographs of the stars and productions illustrate the narrative.	H	6–8	VA	HCC

Focus: B—Biography and autobiography; **C**—Collection of works; **H**—History; **S**—Story; **T**—Techniques or skills; **WC**—World cultures
Related discipline: D—Dance; **E–LA**—English–language arts; **H–SS**—History–social science; **MA**—Mathematics; **MU**—Music; **S**—Science;
  TH—Theatre; **VA**—Visual arts
Framework **component: AP**—Artistic perception; **AV**—Aesthetic valuing; **CE**—Creative expression; **HCC**—Historical and cultural context

◐ Denotes film or videotape

	Focus	Grade level	Related discipline	Framework component
Auch, Mary J. *Glass Slippers Give You Blisters*. New York: Holiday House, 1989.	S	6–8		AV
Several preteens combine their various natural talents to make their school's musical production of *Cinderella* a giant success.				
Bellville, Cheryl. *Theatre Magic: Behind the Scenes at a Children's Theatre*. Minneapolis, Minn.: Carolrhoda, 1986.	S	6–8		AP CE
Opening night of *The Nightingale* is the focus of this book on theatre production. The author tells how the play was created and how the people backstage and onstage work together to create theatre magic.				
Boleslavsky, Richard. *Acting: The First Six Lessons*. New York: Theatre Arts Books, 1987.	T	9–12	E–LA	AP AV
As an actor and director from the Moscow Art Theatre, the author measures the progress of a young actress and offers an interpretation of Stanislavsky's method of acting. This book captures the essence of acting and gives the reader clear views of just what it takes to become an actor or actress.				
Bonanno, Margaret Wander. *Angela Lansbury: A Biography*. New York: St. Martin's, 1987.	B	9–12	H–SS	HCC
This is an in-depth account of both the public and the personal life of the motion picture, Broadway, and television superstar. (Subject matter includes the handling of her children's addictions.)				
Brown, Dee. *Teepee Tales of the American Indian*. New York: Holt, Rinehart and Winston, 1979.	WC	6–8	E–LA	AP HCC
These tales from a variety of Indian tribes are set in times when animals lived as equals with people. The tales could be expanded by students for use in classroom dramatizations.				
Brown, Tricia. *Chinese New Year*. New York: Henry Holt, 1987.	WC	4–5	H–SS	HCC AV
A 5,000-year-old tradition, this ancient spring festival combines many elements associated with today's American holidays. This spirited and informative photo-essay could be used as a guide by students to implement their own celebration.				
Bruder, Melissa. *A Practical Handbook for the Actor*. New York: Vintage, 1986.	T	6–8		AP CE
Developed by a group of young actors, this is a clear, concise guide to "finding a way to live truthfully under the imaginary circumstances of a play."				

Focus: **B**—Biography and autobiography; **C**—Collection of works; **H**—History; **S**—Story; **T**—Techniques or skills; **WC**—World cultures
Related discipline: **D**—Dance; **E–LA**—English–language arts; **H–SS**—History–social science; **MA**—Mathematics; **MU**—Music; **S**—Science; **TH**—Theatre; **VA**—Visual arts
Framework **component:** **AP**—Artistic perception; **AV**—Aesthetic valuing; **CE**—Creative expression; **HCC**—Historical and cultural context

✪ Denotes film or videotape

	Focus	Grade level	Related discipline	Framework component
Burr, Lonnie. *Two for the Show: Great Comedy Teams.* New York: Julian Messner, 1979.	H	9–12		HCC
Famous "show-biz" teams, such as Burns and Allen and the Marx Brothers, are covered in this informative account, with photographs.				
Chambers, Everett. *Producing TV Movies.* New York: Prentice Hall, 1986.	T	6–8	VA	CE
Using his pilot film as a model, the producer-author introduces students to everything that is required of a producer during all stages of production. The appendix contains authentic scripts and other materials that provide a thorough "hands-on" experience.				
Chocolate, Deborah M. Newton. *Kwanzaa.* Chicago: Children's Press, 1990.	WC	4–5	H–SS	HCC
The history and tradition of Kwanzaa, the celebration of kinship that binds the African harvest customs to the cultural and social history of African Americans, is told from one family's perspective. The seven principles of Kwanzaa are highlighted.				
Cockenpot, Marianne. *Eugenio.* Boston: Little, Brown, 1994.	S	K–3	E–LA	AP
Eugenio is left by his poor parents to be raised and cared for by kindly circus folk. One day, after becoming the most popular clown under the big top, he refuses to perform. Only the fortune-teller, Madame Cobra, can help him. Lorenzo Mattoti is the illustrator.				
Cooney, Barbara. *Miss Rumphius.* New York: Viking, 1982.	S	K–3	E–LA	AP
Great Aunt Alice Rumphius travels to wonderful faraway places. But she needs time to figure out how to fulfill her grandfather's request "to make the world more beautiful." When interpreting this story for creative drama, children can play out their ideas for making the world more beautiful before sharing those of Miss Rumphius.				
Currell, David. *The Complete Book of Puppet Theatre.* London: A and C Black, 1985.	T	9–12	VA	CE
This comprehensive book about making and performing with puppets is an excellent teachers' resource for all levels.				
Dalgliesh, Alice. *The Courage of Sarah Noble.* New York: Macmillan, 1986.	S	4–5	H–SS	HCC
In this true story Sarah travels into the Connecticut wilds and spends time with an American Indian family. It is a charming tale of courage, faith, and friendship.				

Focus: B—Biography and autobiography; **C**—Collection of works; **H**—History; **S**—Story; **T**—Techniques or skills; **WC**—World cultures
Related discipline: D—Dance; **E–LA**—English–language arts; **H–SS**—History–social science; **MA**—Mathematics; **MU**—Music; **S**—Science; **TH**—Theatre. **VA**—Visual arts
Framework **component: AP**—Artistic perception; **AV**—Aesthetic valuing; **CE**—Creative expression; **HCC**—Historical and cultural context

⦿ Denotes film or videotape

	Focus	Grade level	Related discipline	Framework component
DePaola, Tomie. *Strega Nona*. Englewood Cliffs, N.J.: Prentice Hall, 1975.	S	6–8	E–LA	AP
Strega Nona, "Grandma Witch," goes away, leaving her helper, Big Anthony, in charge. Big Anthony is intrigued by the big pasta pot. He is able to start the pot, but not to stop it. Disaster is averted in the nick of time.				
DePaola, Tomie. *When Everyone Was Fast Asleep*. New York: Holiday House, 1976.	S	K–3	E–LA	AP
Two children are awakened by the Fog Maiden's cat and are taken away to an enchanted world where they have a night of adventure before returning home.				
De Veaux, Alexis. *An Enchanted Tale*. New York: Harper and Row, 1987.	S	K–3	E–LA	AP
This tale of a young boy and his enchanted hair is about being different and being yourself. A rich story with vivid black-and-white drawings, it would easily translate into drama.				
Dolch, Edward W., and Marguerite P. Dolch. *Stories from Japan*. Champaign, Ill.: Garrard, 1960.	WC	6–8	H–SS	HCC
This collection of folktales includes some that are rich with potential for dramatizing, such as "Momotaro, the Peach Boy," "Little One-Inch," and "Urashimo."				
Dowd, Ned. *That's a Wrap: How Movies Are Made*. New York: Simon and Schuster, 1991.	T	4–5	VA	HCC AV
In this unique look at the creation of a motion picture, on-the-spot photographs give a bird's-eye view of the processes of make-up, wardrobe, lighting, and special effects.				
Edelson, Edward. *Great Monsters of the Movies*. New York: Doubleday, 1973.	H	9–12	E–LA	HCC
Vampires and zombies share space with Frankenstein and King Kong in this popular work. Also see Edelson's *Funny Men of the Movies*.				
Ende, Michael. *Ophelia's Shadow Theatre*. Translated from the German by Anthea Bell. New York: Overlook Press, 1989.	S	K–3		AV
Miss Ophelia teaches abandoned shadows the plays she learned as a theatre prompter. The wonderful illustrations capture the sense of mystery conveyed by the text.				
Gackenbach, Dick. *Harry and the Terrible Whatzit*. New York: Clarion, 1984.	S	K–3	E–LA	CE
A courageous young boy is forced to face his greatest fear, and he overcomes it. This story could easily be expanded for drama or rewritten to reflect other fears of children.				

Focus: B—Biography and autobiography; **C**—Collection of works; **H**—History; **S**—Story; **T**—Techniques or skills; **WC**—World cultures
Related discipline: D—Dance; **E–LA**—English-language arts; **H–SS**—History–social science; **MA**—Mathematics; **MU**—Music; **S**—Science; **TH**—Theatre; **VA**—Visual arts
Framework **component: AP**—Artistic perception; **AV**—Aesthetic valuing; **CE**—Creative expression; **HCC**—Historical and cultural context

✪ Denotes film or videotape

	Focus	Grade level	Related discipline	Framework component
Gackenbach, Dick. *The Leatherman.* New York: Clarion, 1977.	S	4–5	H–SS	HCC
This intriguing tale is based on the life of an actual American eccentric. The line illustrations fully capture the emotions of the curious yet anxious boy. The story could easily be translated into a classroom drama.				
Gelber, Carol. *Masks Tell Stories (Beyond Museum Walls).* Brookfield, Conn.: Millbrook, 1993.	WC	4–5	VA	HCC
The author traces the societal significance of masks in tribal ceremonies, the theatre, and everyday life.				
Geras, Adele. *Happy Endings.* New York: Harcourt Brace, 1991.	S	9–12	E–LA	AV
In this entertaining depiction of the backstage "dramas" in the theatre, the themes of Chekhov's *Three Sisters* are mirrored in the relationships among the play's actors.				
Gillmore, Kate. *Jason and the Bard.* New York: Houghton Mifflin, 1993.	S	6–8	E–LA	HCC
A young man spends his summer as an intern with the Avon Shakespeare Festival in the hope of learning the craft of his passion—acting. This thorough depiction of the theatre is combined with minor mystery and romance. See also Gillmore's *Enter Three Witches* and *Remembrance of the Sun.*				
Goodall, John S. *Midnight Adventures of Kelly, Dot, and Esmerelda.* New York: Atheneum, 1972.	S	6–8	VA	AP
Three toys come to life at midnight. They climb into a painting, which also becomes real, and have a series of adventures. This is a wordless story told through paintings. Children could add ideas for additional adventures.				
Green, Lila. *Tales from Hispanic Lands.* Morristown, N.J.: Silver Burdett, 1979.	WC	6–8	E–LA	HCC AV
This book, which contains nine tales from Spain, South America, Mexico, and Puerto Rico, provides rich source material for students to translate into creative drama.				
Hall, Irina. *Boxman.* New York: Viking, 1992.	S	K–3	VA	AP
Inspired to be different, a little boy uses a cardboard box to create Boxman. Colorfully illustrated, this story is suitable for student dramatization.				

Focus: **B**—Biography and autobiography; **C**—Collection of works; **H**—History; **S**—Story; **T**—Techniques or skills; **WC**—World cultures
Related discipline: **D**—Dance; **E–LA**—English-language arts; **H–SS**—History-social science; **MA**—Mathematics; **MU**—Music; **S**—Science; **TH**—Theatre; **VA**—Visual arts
Framework **component:** **AP**—Artistic perception; **AV**—Aesthetic valuing; **CE**—Creative expression; **HCC**—Historical and cultural context
✪ Denotes film or videotape

	Focus	Grade level	Related discipline	Framework component
Hall, Robin. *Three Tales from Japan.* New Orleans, La.: Anchorage Press, 1973.	WC	6–8	E–LA	HCC
The dramatized folktales include "The Magic Fan," "The Princess of the Sea," and "Little Peach Boy." Although they are intended to be produced by adults for children, older children would enjoy the challenge of acting out these tales.				
Hargrove, Jim. *Steven Spielberg: Amazing Filmmaker.* Chicago, Ill.: Children's Press, 1988.	B	6–8	VA	HCC
This lively biography discusses many of Spielberg's early works, including *E.T., Jaws, Poltergeist,* and *Back to the Future.* Included are photographs from the filming of *Jaws, Indiana Jones,* and *Close Encounters of the Third Kind.*				
Hill, Elizabeth Starr. *Curtain Going Up.* New York: Viking, 1995.	S	6–8	E–LA	AP
Fritzi learns that being a star sometimes doesn't have anything to do with the work one does. She's back on stage but finds that ambition often gets in the way of loyalty.				
Hodgman, Ann. *A Day in the Life of a Theater Set Designer.* New York: Troll Associates, 1988.	T	4–5		AP
By spotlighting individuals engaged in their daily work, the author presents a close-up look at what their jobs entail.				
Hoffman, Mary. *Amazing Grace.* New York: Dial, 1991.	S	K–3	E–LA AV	HCC
This is an inspiring tale of a young African-American girl whose classmates proclaim that she cannot play Peter Pan in their production of that play because she is black and female. Beautiful watercolor illustrations that jump off the page bring passion to the story.				
Holmes, Barbara W. *Charlotte Shakespeare and Annie the Great.* New York: HarperCollins, 1989.	S	4–5	E–LA	AP
In this book, the third in a series featuring the character Charlotte Cheetham, Charlotte writes a Halloween play for her sixth grade class, and her best friend Annie plays the lead. See also Charlotte the Starlet.				
Houghton, Norris. *Entrances and Exits: A Life in and out of the Theatre.* New York: Limelight Editions, 1991.	B	9–12	H–SS	HCC
The memoirs of this director, set designer, producer, author, and educator span a career of over 50 years, a fantastic journey crisscrossed by encounters with some of the most notable figures of the twentieth century.				
Howe, James. *Stage Fright.* New York: Macmillan, 1986.	S	4–5		AP
Young sleuth Sebastian Bart must solve a theatrical mystery set in a summer stock production.				

Focus: B—Biography and autobiography; **C**—Collection of works; **H**—History; **S**—Story; **T**—Techniques or skills; **WC**—World cultures
Related discipline: D—Dance; **E–LA**—English–language arts; **H–SS**—History–social science; **MA**—Mathematics; **MU**—Music; **S**—Science;
   TH—Theatre; **VA**—Visual arts
Framework **component: AP**—Artistic perception; **AV**—Aesthetic valuing; **CE**—Creative expression; **HCC**—Historical and cultural context

✪ Denotes film or videotape

	Focus	Grade level	Related discipline	Framework component

Huberman, Caryn, and Jo Anne Wetzel. *Onstage/Backstage.* Minneapolis, Minn.: Carolrhoda Books, 1987.

| S | 6–8 | E–LA | AP |

Through black-and-white and color photographs, a ten-year-old actress tells about her association with the Palo Alto Children's Theatre, the oldest children's theatre in the United States, and about her performance in Kipling's *Just So Stories.*

Jagendorf, Mortiz, and Virginia Weng. *The Magic Boat and Other Chinese Folk Stories.* New York: Vanguard, 1980.

| WC | 4–5 | H–SS | HCC |

These folktales from the People's Republic of China reflect the land's many minorities and the cultural history of the people. They constitute a rich resource for creative drama experiences.

Johnson, Dolores. *The Best Bug to Be.* New York: Macmillan, 1992.

| S | K–3 | | AV |

Kelly does not receive a starring role in the school play. Instead, she is cast as a bumblebee and teased by her classmates. With practice and encouragement, Kelly steals the show and becomes the envy of her class.

Keats, Ezra. John Henry*: An American Legend.* New York: Knopf, 1987.

| S | K–3 | MU | CE |

This story of the legendary "steel-driving man" who "died with a hammer in his hand" could be performed interactively, with some children performing the rhythmic noises of the hammer and others the locomotive.

Leigh, Vanora. *Elvis Presley.* New York: Bookwright, 1986.

| B | 4–5 | MU | HCC |

This easy-to-read biography chronicles the rags-to-riches story of Elvis Presley, the rock 'n' roll superstar who also made over 25 movies.

Lemieux, Michele. *The Pied Piper of Hamelin.* New York: Morrow, 1993.

| S | 4–5 | E–LA | AP HCC |

The story of the piper who lures the rats and, ultimately, the children, from the city of Hamelin is retold with beautiful illustrations by the author. See also Lemieux's *Peter and the Wolf.*

Lindsey, David L. *The Wonderful Chirrionera and Other Tales from Mexican Folklore.* Austin, Tex.: Heidelberg, 1974.

| WC | 4–5 | VA | HCC |

Droll stories with imaginative endings are accompanied by striking woodcuts by Barbara Mathews Whitehead.

Focus: **B**—Biography and autobiography; **C**—Collection of works; **H**—History; **S**—Story; **T**—Techniques or skills; **WC**—World cultures
Related discipline: **D**—Dance; **E–LA**—English-language arts; **H–SS**—History–social science; **MA**—Mathematics; **MU**—Music; **S**—Science; **TH**—Theatre; **VA**—Visual arts
Framework **component:** **AP**—Artistic perception; **AV**—Aesthetic valuing; **CE**—Creative expression; **HCC**—Historical and cultural context

⊙ Denotes film or videotape

	Focus	Grade level	Related discipline	Framework component
McNamara, Brooks. *The Shuberts of Broadway.* New York: Oxford, 1990.	B	9–12	H–SS	HCC
Drawn from a collection of primary source material at the Shubert Archive, this biography re-creates the lives of Broadway legends Sam, Lee, and J. J. Shubert. The lively text is accompanied by over 200 illustrations.				
McPhail, David. *First Flight.* Boston: Joy Street Books/ Little, Brown, 1987.	S	K–3	E–LA	CE
Playful illustrations accompany this account of a fictional little boy and his unusual companion on their first airline flight. It is easily expanded for use as instructional drama.				
McTigue, Mary. *Acting like a Pro.* Crozet, Va.: Betterway Publications, 1992.	T	9–12	VA	CE
The author reveals the tips and techniques used by the professionals from auditions to opening nights.				
Mar, S. Y. Lu. *Chinese Tales of Folklore.* New York: Criterion, 1964.	WC	6–8	H–SS	HCC
In this collection of ancient Chinese stories, historical notes precede each story and relate each tale to a specific period and to real people of the past.				
Maychick, Diana. *Meryl Streep: The Reluctant Superstar.* New York: St. Martin's, 1984.	B	6–8	H–SS	HCC
This biography weaves a warm narrative with personal interviews of Miss Streep and those she has worked with. It is a tribute to the actress, who refuses to sacrifice her moral and artistic standards for fame and fortune.				
Millerson, Gerald. *TV Lighting Methods.* New York: Prentice Hall, 1986.	S T	9–12	VA	AP CE
For those students involved in television or video productions, this book provides invaluable advice on how to produce the perfect light to show exactly what the audience must see. See also *Millerson's TV Scenic Design Handbook.*				
Mostin, Doug. *Coming to Terms with Acting: An Instructive Glossary.* New York: Drama Book Publishers, 1994.	T	9–12	E–LA	AP CE
The terminology that is used in teaching and directing actors is defined in this book. An overview of how each term is used in theatre is also included. This book is appropriate for both students and teachers.				

Focus: **B**—Biography and autobiography; **C**—Collection of works; **H**—History; **S**—Story; **T**—Techniques or skills; **WC**—World cultures
Related discipline: **D**—Dance; **E–LA**—English–language arts; **H–SS**—History–social science; **MA**—Mathematics; **MU**—Music; **S**—Science; **TH**—Theatre; **VA**—Visual arts
Framework **component:** **AP**—Artistic perception; **AV**—Aesthetic valuing; **CE**—Creative expression; **HCC**—Historical and cultural context

✪ Denotes film or videotape

	Focus	Grade level	Related discipline	Framework component
North, Jack. *Arnold Schwarzenegger.* New York: Dillon, 1994. This is a colorful biography of the Austrian-born bodybuilder's rise to fame and superstardom as an action-adventure movie hero. Attention is also given to Schwarzenegger's humanitarian side.	B	4–5		HCC
Perlman, Marc. *Movie Classics.* Minneapolis, Minn.: Lerner, 1992. The author discusses seven movie classics, including, *Gone with the Wind, Psycho,* and *The Godfather* series, showing how these films have changed movie history.	H	6–8	H–SS	HCC
Politi, Leo. *Mr. Fong's Toy Shop.* New York: Scribner, 1978. In preparing children of his village to celebrate the Moon Festival, Mr. Fong shows them how to make puppets. The author's illustrations enliven the story.	S	K–3	E–LA VA	AP
Pryor, Nick. *Putting on a Play.* New York: Thompson Learning, 1994. This book is a guide for children wanting to produce and direct a play themselves. Readers are taken through all the necessary steps: script selection, auditions, rehearsals, makeup and costumes, publicity, tickets, and, finally, the performance.	T	4–5		CE
Ratliff, Gerald Lee, and Suzanne Trauth. *On Stage: Producing Musical Theatre.* New York: Rosen Publishing Group, 1988. This is an enthusiastic and informative introduction to acting in, directing, and producing musicals. Also included are black-and-white stills from various college productions and examples from well known musicals	T	9–12	MU	CE
Rosenberg, Robert. *Bill Cosby: The Changing Black Image.* Brookfield, Conn.: Millbrook, 1991. This biography of comedian Bill Cosby explains how his personal form of humor helped move African Americans into the mainstream of U.S. entertainment.	B	9–12	H–SS	HCC
Ross, Stewart. *Shakespeare and Macbeth: The Story Behind the Play.* New York: Viking, 1994. Current historical findings and contemporary critical thinking are combined to re-create Shakespeare's writing of *Macbeth,* the actors who originally performed it, and the economic worries of the time.	H	4–5	H–SS	HCC

Focus: B—Biography and autobiography; **C**—Collection of works; **H**—History; **S**—Story; **T**—Techniques or skills; **WC**—World cultures
Related discipline: D—Dance; **E–LA**—English–language arts; **H–SS**—History–social science; **MA**—Mathematics; **MU**—Music; **S**—Science; **TH**—Theatre; **VA**—Visual arts
Framework **component: AP**—Artistic perception; **AV**—Aesthetic valuing; **CE**—Creative expression; **HCC**—Historical and cultural context

✪ Denotes film or videotape

	Focus	Grade level	Related discipline	Framework component

Shakespeare, William. *The Tempest.* Retold by Bruce Coville. New York: Bantam Doubleday, 1994.

| | S | 6–8 | E–LA | HCC |

This is a simplified prose retelling of Shakespeare's play about the exiled Duke of Milan, who uses his magical powers to confront his enemies on an enchanted island. Beautiful paintings by Ruth Sanderson illustrate the text.

Showers, Paul. *How to Talk.* New York: HarperCollins, 1992.

| | T | K–3 | VA | AP |

This clear and inviting introduction to sounds and speech will help young dramatists become more aware of their breathing and speaking.

Shute, Linda. *Momotaro the Peach Boy: A Traditional Japanese Tale.* New York: Lothrop, Lee and Shepard, 1986.

| | WC | 4–5 | H–SS | HCC |

With illustrations that add a touch of the grace and pageantry of medieval Japan, this traditional Japanese folktale is rich with drama.

Spolin, Viola. *Improvisation for the Theatre.* Evanston, Ill.: Northwestern University Press, 1983.

| | T | 9–12 | | CE |

Designed for use by students and teachers, this guidebook focuses on a theory of teaching and directing theatre. A series of classroom exercises and activities is included that would be appropriate for grade levels five through twelve.

Spotlight on Movie Stars. Austin, Tex.: Steck-Vaughn, 1992.

| | B | 4–5 | | HCC |

Eight short biographies are presented in a magazine-style format with numerous quotes and large colorful photographs. Biographies of Michael J. Fox, Whoopi Goldberg, and Tom Cruise are included. See also *Spotlight on TV Stars,* featuring, among others, Kirk Cameron and John Stamos.

Stanley, Diane, and Peter Vennema. *Bard of Avon.* New York: Morrow Junior Books, 1992.

| | B | 4–5 | E–LA H–SS | HCC |

This picture-book biography provides a historically accurate look at the world's most famous playwright. Imaginative full-color illustrations grab the reader's attention.

Staskowski, Andréa. *Movie Musicals.* Minneapolis, Minn.: Lerner, 1992.

| | H | 6–8 | MU | HCC |

Film instructor Andréa Staskowski discusses several important musicals, including *Singin' in the Rain, West Side Story,* and *Dirty Dancing,* to show how musicals have evolved over time.

Focus: B—Biography and autobiography; **C**—Collection of works; **H**—History; **S**—Story; **T**—Techniques or skills; **WC**—World cultures
Related discipline: D—Dance; **E–LA**—English-language arts; **H–SS**—History–social science; **MA**—Mathematics; **MU**—Music; **S**—Science; **TH**—Theatre; **VA**—Visual arts
***Framework* component: AP**—Artistic perception; **AV**—Aesthetic valuing; **CE**—Creative expression; **HCC**—Historical and cultural context

○ Denotes film or videotape

	Focus	Grade level	Related discipline	Framework component

Strasberg, Lee. *A Dream of Passion: The Development of the Method*. Boston: Little, Brown, 1987.

> Drawing from a lifetime of directing, acting, and teaching, the leading American teacher of "the Method" describes his ideas on the theatre and the training of actors.

B — 9–12 — — HCC

Tadjo, Véronique. *Lord of the Dance: An African Retelling*. New York: Lippincott, 1988.

> This poem tells the story of the Senufo people and is illustrated in the style of Senufo art. The Lord of the Dance, in the well-known English hymn, has become the mask worshipped by the Senufo.

WC — 4–5 — H–SS — HCC

Thurman, Judith, and David Jonathan. *The Magic Lantern: How Movies Got to Move*. New York: Atheneum, 1978.

> One thousand years ago the Chinese developed the concept of making still images appear to move. This history of early moviemaking tells that story and many others.

H — 6–8 — VA — HCC

Vennema, Peter. *Bard of Avon: The Story of William Shakespeare*. New York: Morrow Junior Books, 1992.

> This story of William Shakespeare evokes the dramatic world of the Elizabethan era in which he lived and created.

S — K–3 — VA — HCC

Viorst, Judith. *Alexander Who Used to Be Rich Last Sunday*. New York: Macmillan (Aladdin), 1987.

> Alexander is left with only bus tokens after he finds a day's worth of things to spend his money on.

S — K 3 — E–LA — CE

Warren, Lee. *The Theatre of Africa*. New York: Prentice Hall, 1975.

> This overview of various theatre forms in Africa includes formal theatre, storytelling, puppetry, and other forms. It is clearly written and uses photographs and discussions of major playwrights to tell its story.

WC — 9–12 — H–SS — HCC

Williams, Michael. *Crocodile Burning*. New York: Dutton Children's Books, 1992.

> Seraki, a South African teenager, has witnessed hatred and violence his entire life. By joining the cast of a local musical, he is able to forget his fears and travel to America. As the story unfolds, readers gain a detailed account of what it takes to put on a production.

WC — 6–8 — H–SS — HCC

Wyndham, Robert. *Tales the People Tell in China*. New York: Julian Messner, 1971.

> Classic illustrations grace this book of stories based on old tales written for contemporary children. The tales reflect all levels of Chinese society, customs, and religion.

WC — 4–5 — E–LA — HCC

Focus: B—Biography and autobiography; **C**—Collection of works; **H**—History; **S**—Story; **T**—Techniques or skills; **WC**—World cultures

Related discipline: D—Dance; **E–LA**—English–language arts; **H–SS**—History–social science; **MA**—Mathematics; **MU**—Music; **S**—Science; **TH**—Theatre; **VA**—Visual arts

Framework **component: AP**—Artistic perception; **AV**—Aesthetic valuing; **CE**—Creative expression; **HCC**—Historical and cultural context

✪ Denotes film or videotape

Visual Arts

	Focus	Grade level	Related discipline	Framework component
Alcorn, Johnny. *Rembrandt's Beret.* New York: Tambourine, 1993.	S	K–3	H–SS	HCC
Beautifully illustrated by Stephen Alcorn, this book is a magical story of a young boy who discovers the Hall of the Old Masters in Florence, Italy, and finds his path as an artist.				
Aliki. *A Medieval Feast.* New York: Harper and Row, 1983.	S	K–3	H–SS	HCC
Camdenton Manor prepares for a night of feasting, dance, and song with the king in this beautifully illustrated book.				
Anderson, Bjork. *Linnea in Monet's Garden.* New York: R and S Books, 1985.	B	6–8	H–SS	HCC
When Linnea visits Claude Monet's garden in Giverny, she gets to stand on the bridge over his lily pond and walk through his house. Later, when she sees his paintings in Paris, she understands what it means for a painter to be called an impressionist. This delightful book contains photographs of Monet's paintings as well as old family snapshots.				
"Animals in Art," *Faces: The Magazine About People.* New York: Cobblestone Publishing, January, 1995.	H	4–5	H–SS	HCC
This issue looks at how animals are represented in different cultures and regions: the ancient Andes, the European Renaissance, Africa, and Eastern Asia.				
Arnold, Tedd. *The Signmaker's Assistant.* New York: Dial, 1992.	S	4–5	E–LA	AV
A young signmaker's apprentice dreams of having his own sign shop but creates havoc when he is left in charge by himself.				
Arnosky, Jim. *Near the Sea.* New York: Lothrop, Lee and Shepard, 1990.	S	4–5	S	AP
Through a journey to the sea, the author and artist guide us through scenes of the seashore in beautifully illustrated oil paintings.				
Ash, Russell, and Bernard Highton. *Aesop's Fables: A Classic Illustrated Edition.* New York: Chronicle Books, 1990.	S	4–5	E–LA	HCC
A collection of art spanning the last century complements these famous tales.				
Avi-Yonah, Michael. *Piece by Piece! Mosaics of the Ancient World.* Minneapolis, Minn.: Lerner, 1993.	H	6–8	H–SS	HCC
This book describes ancient and modern mosaic techniques as well as early Greek, Roman, and Byzantine mosaics.				

Focus: B—Biography and autobiography; **C**—Collection of works; **H**—History; **S**—Story; **T**—Techniques or skills; **WC**—World cultures
Related discipline: D—Dance; **E–LA**—English–language arts; **H–SS**—History–social science; **MA**—Mathematics; **MU**—Music; **S**—Science; **TH**—Theatre; **VA**—Visual arts
Framework **component: AP**—Artistic perception; **AV**—Aesthetic valuing; **CE**—Creative expression; **HCC**—Historical and cultural context

✪ Denotes film or videotape

	Focus	Grade level	Related discipline	Framework component
Baker, Alan. *White Rabbit's Color Book*. New York: Kingfisher, 1994. White Rabbit hops from one paint pot to another, changing colors as he goes, until he ends up covered with a mixture of all colors.	S	K–3		AP
Bang, Molly Garrett. *Tye May and the Magic Brush*. New York: Mulberry, 1981. With the aid of a magic brush, a poor Chinese girl is able to realize her dreams of becoming a painter, inspiring those around her.	WC	4–5	H–SS	HCC
Baylor, Byrd, and Tom Bahti. *When Clay Sings*. New York: Macmillan (Aladdin), 1972. This Caldecott Honor Book describes the symbols on ancient clay pots designed by Native Americans and tells the stories associated with these symbols.	WC	6–8	H–SS E–LA	HCC
Beatty, Patricia. *O the Red Rose Tree*. New York: Morrow Junior Books, 1972. In 1893 four girls befriend an old lady and try to find seven shades of red for the special quilt she wants to make. The scarcity of the quilting materials and the enormity of the search don't stop Amanda from promising to make her friend's dream finally come true.	S	6–8	E–LA H–SS	HCC
Bennett, Cathereen. *Will Rogers: Quotable Cowboy*. Minneapolis, Minn.: Runestone Press, 1995. With the possible exception of Mark Twain, no humorist has captured the hearts of Americans more than Will Rogers. He took his skills to Broadway and was featured in several films, his own newspaper column, and a radio show before his death in an airplane crash at the age of fifty-six.	B	4–5	H–SS	HCC
Bolton, Jane. *My Grandmother's Patchwork Quilt*. New York: Delacorte, 1994. The author describes the quilt made by her grandmother, with photographs and a narrative about each block. Also included are instructions and patterns for making a quilt.	S	4–5		AP HCC
Brown, Marcia. *Shadow*. New York: Scribner's, 1982. The many images of shadow are brought into being, changed, hidden, and magically captured with fascination and suspense in this African story.	WC	K–3	H–SS	HCC

Focus: **B**—Biography and autobiography; **C**—Collection of works; **H**—History; **S**—Story; **T**—Techniques or skills; **WC**—World cultures
Related discipline: **D**—Dance; **E–LA**—English-language arts; **H–SS**—History–social science; **MA**—Mathematics; **MU**—Music; **S**—Science; **TH**—Theatre; **VA**—Visual arts
Framework **component:** **AP**—Artistic perception; **AV**—Aesthetic valuing; **CE**—Creative expression; **HCC**—Historical and cultural context
✪ Denotes film or videotape

	Focus	Grade level	Related discipline	Framework component
Brust, Beth Wagner. *The Amazing Paper Cuttings of Hans Christian Andersen.* New York: Ticknor and Fields, 1994.	H	9–12	E–LA	AP HCC
The author tells the story of Andersen as an artist who used his many talents to escape the poverty into which he was born. Often he made paper cuttings while he was telling a fairy tale; then he gave them to the children listening.				
Capek, Michael. *Artistic Trickery: The Tradition of Trompe L'Oeil Art.* Minneapolis, Minn.: Lerner, 1995.	H	6–8	H–SS	AP HCC
From the ancient Greeks to contemporary designers, artists have been inspired to play visual jokes. This book lets the reader in on the gags.				
Carle, Eric. *Draw Me a Star.* New York: Philomel, 1992.	S	4–5	E–LA	AP
This is the story of an artist who, as a child, begins to draw single but meaningful shapes that have an impact on his life. Dramatic fingerpaint collage prints illustrate the text.				
Castaneda, Omar. *Abuela's Weave.* New York: Lee and Low, 1993.	WC	4–5	H–SS	HCC
A young Guatemalan girl and her grandmother grow closer as they weave some special creations and then make a trip to the market in hopes of selling them. This book is also published in Spanish.				
Cech, John. *Jacques-Henri Lartigue: Boy with a Camera.* New York: Four Winds, 1994.	B	4–5	H–SS	HCC
Remarkable photographs and text tell about Lartigue's accomplishments at an early age. He began taking photographs in 1902 at age seven and pioneered the age of photography.				
Celebrate America in Poetry and Art. Edited by Nora Panzer. New York: Hyperion, 1994.	C	9–12	E–LA	HCC AV
This collection of American poetry that celebrates more than 200 years of American life and history is illustrated by fine art from the collection of the National Museum of American Art. For instance, the painting *Construction of the Dam,* by William Gropper, is paired with the poem "I Hear America Singing," by Walt Whitman, and the poem "I, Too," by Langston Hughes.				
Chief Seattle. *Brother Eagle, Sister Sky: A Message from Chief Seattle.* New York: Dial, 1991.	S	4–5	E–LA	AP HCC
A Suquamish Indian chief describes his people's respect and love for the earth and their concern about its destruction. The beautiful ink drawings by Susan Jeffers enhance the text.				

Focus: B—Biography and autobiography; **C**—Collection of works; **H**—History; **S**—Story; **T**—Techniques or skills; **WC**—World cultures

Related discipline: D—Dance; **E–LA**—English–language arts; **H–SS**—History–social science; **MA**—Mathematics; **MU**—Music; **S**—Science; **TH**—Theatre; **VA**—Visual arts

Framework **component: AP**—Artistic perception; **AV**—Aesthetic valuing; **CE**—Creative expression; **HCC**—Historical and cultural context

✪ Denotes film or videotape

	Focus	Grade level	Related discipline	Framework component
Clément, Claude. *The Painter and the Wild Swans.* New York: Dial, 1989.	WC	4–5	E–LA	HCC AV
An artist wonders how he can ever hope to capture the beauty of a flock of wild swans. Acrylic paintings and Japanese calligraphy complement the text.				
Collins, Pat Lowery. *I Am an Artist.* Brookfield, Conn.: Millbrook, 1992.	S	K–3	E–LA	AP
In this book, beautifully illustrated by Robin Brickwau, the author teaches us that we are all artists through our perceptions of life and the surrounding world.				
Conner, Patrick. *People at Home.* New York: Atheneum, 1982.	WC	6–8	H–SS	AP HCC
The author examines the way artists in different countries and in various historical periods portray people in their homes. See also Conner's *People at Work.*				
Cooke, Jean. *Costumes and Clothes.* New York: Bookwright, 1987.	H	6–8	H–SS	AP
Photographs and brief narratives show clothes as they relate to climate, fashion, work, religion, and tradition.				
Cuneo, Mary Louise. *How to Grow a Picket Fence.* New York: HarperCollins, 1993.	S	4–5	DR E–LA	AP
A child uses a basket of sticks, some daisy pudding, and sun-dried socks to grow a picket fence. The colorful illustrations by Nadine Bernard Westcott heighten the fantasy.				
Czernecki, Stefan, and Timothy Rhodes. *Nina's Treasures.* New York: Sterling, 1990.	S	6–8	H–SS	HCC
When Katherina runs out of food at the end of winter, her beloved hen Nina saves them both by laying marvelous multicolored eggs. The illustrations by Czernecki are in a beautiful Eastern European style.				
Davidson, Rosemary. *Take a Look: An Introduction to the Experience of Art.* New York: Penguin, 1993.	H	6–8	H–SS	AP HCC
This book introduces the history, techniques, and functions of art through discussion and reproductions of paintings, photographs, drawings, and design elements. It also includes valuable diagrams and information about seeing and looking at art.				
Davol, Marguerite W. *The Heart of the Wood.* Simon and Schuster, 1992.	S	K–3	MU	AP
Illustrations and poetry follow the transformation of a tree where a mockingbird sings into a fiddle that captures the tree's music.				

Focus: B—Biography and autobiography; **C**—Collection of works; **H**—History; **S**—Story; **T**—Techniques or skills; **WC**—World cultures
Related discipline: D—Dance; **E–LA**—English–language arts; **H–SS**—History–social science; **MA**—Mathematics; **MU**—Music; **S**—Science; **TH**—Theatre; **VA**—Visual arts
***Framework* component: AP**—Artistic perception; **AV**—Aesthetic valuing; **CE**—Creative expression; **HCC**—Historical and cultural context

✪ Denotes film or videotape

	Focus	Grade level	Related discipline	Framework component
Demarest, Chris. *Lindbergh.* New York: Crown, 1993. The early life of Charles Lindbergh, leading up to his history-making transatlantic flight in 1927, is described in this biography. The watercolor illustrations reveal an artist with great control of the medium.	B	4–5	H–SS S	HCC
de Mejo, Oscar. *La Bella Magellona and the Little Cavalier.* New York: Philomel, 1992. Big-footed Magellona loves the little Cavalier, who is so tiny that he goes for rides on her dog, but their love is doomed until they discover magic in the waters at two nearby lakes. Energetic illustrations enrich the text.	S	4–5	E–LA	AV
de Mejo, Oscar. *Oscar de Mejo's ABC.* HarperCollins, 1992. The renowned painter renders each letter of the alphabet as a symbol of a person, place, or thing.	T	K–3	H–SS	AP
DePaola, Tomie. *The Art Lesson.* New York: Putnam, 1989. Tommy wants to be an artist and waits patiently until first grade, when the art teacher comes to his classroom. He finds that the pictures he draws on his own show his independence.	S	K–3	E–LA	AV
DePaola, Tomie. *The Legend of the Indian Paintbrush.* New York: Putnam, 1988. Little Gopher has a dream vision that leads him to paint a picture that "is as pure as the colors in the evening sky."	WC	K–3	H–SS E–LA	AP HCC
Dowd, Ned. *That's a Wrap: How Movies Are Made.* New York: Simon and Schuster, 1991. The many steps involved in developing and filming a motion picture and preparing it for release are described in this book. Photographs of a movie crew on location enhance the text.	T	6–8	DR	AP CE
Drucker, Malka. *Frida Kahlo: Torment and Triumph in Her Life.* New York: Bantam, 1991. This candid biography of the tormented and renowned Mexican artist includes reproductions and photographs of her paintings and her life with Diego Rivera.	B	9–12	H–SS	HCC
Edwards, Michelle. *A Baker's Portrait.* New York: Lothrop, Lee and Shepard, 1991. A young painter learns to see beyond physical appearance in rendering portraits of her relatives.	S	K–3	E–LA	AV
Edwards, Michelle. *Eve and Smithy.* New York: Lothrop, Lee and Shepard, 1994. Smithy tries to think of a gift for Eve, his neighbor who gardens and paints pictures of Iowa.	S	4–5	E–LA	AP

Focus: B—Biography and autobiography; **C**—Collection of works; **H**—History; **S**—Story; **T**—Techniques or skills; **WC**—World cultures
Related discipline: D—Dance; **E–LA**—English–language arts; **H–SS**—History–social science; **MA**—Mathematics; **MU**—Music; **S**—Science; **TH**—Theatre; **VA**—Visual arts
Framework **component: AP**—Artistic perception; **AV**—Aesthetic valuing; **CE**—Creative expression; **HCC**—Historical and cultural context

○ Denotes film or videotape

	Focus	Grade level	Related discipline	Framework component
Ehrlich, Amy. *Lucy's Winter Tale.* New York: Dial, 1992.	S	4–5	DR	AP
Lucy is kidnapped by Ivan the juggler, who includes her in his miniature circus as he travels to a new town in search of his sweetheart, Martina. Full-page acrylic paintings enhance the text and can be used to illustrate skill and techniques in painting.				
EYEWITNESS ART. New York: Dorling Kindersley, 1993.	H B	9–12	H–SS	HCC AV
This series of books, including volumes on Gauguin, impressionism, Manet, Monet, perspective, van Gogh, watercolor, Goya, postimpressionism, and color, speaks with beauty, authority, and impact through the words of a variety of artists; and photographs of artists, monuments, and techniques. Photographs of letters, palettes, clothing, and influential items from popular culture are integrated into the text.				
✪ *Faith Ringgold: The Last Story Quilt.* L & S Video Enterprises, n.d. Order from Arts America, 9 Benedict Place, Greenwich, CT 06830, (800) 553-5278.	B	9–12		AP HCC
This film, created and produced by Linda Freeman, is an insider's look at how one woman, through patience, perseverance, and education, has fulfilled her dream of becoming an artist.				
Feelings, Tom. *Soul Looks Back in Wonder.* New York: Dial, 1993.	C	4–5	E–LA	AP HCC
Artwork by Feelings and poems by such writers as Maya Angelou, Langston Hughes, and Askia M. Toure portray the creativity, strength, and beauty of their African-American heritage.				
Feiffer, Jules. *The Man in the Ceiling.* New York: HarperCollins, 1993.	S	6–8	E–LA	AV
Jimmy, who longs to be a cartoonist, learns that he can find acceptance by pursuing what he knows how to do best. The drawings capture the spirit of this story and its characters.				
Florian, Douglas. *A Painter.* New York: Greenwillow, 1993.	T	K–3	E–LA	AP CE
The author briefly describes the painter's tools, subject matter, and feelings while creating a work of art. The vivid watercolor and colored-pencil illustrations tell the story, with minimum text.				
Freedman, Russell. *Buffalo Hunt.* New York: Holiday House, 1988.	H B	6–8	H–SS	HCC
Paintings and drawings by artists George Catlin and Karl Bodmer, who traveled the West in the 1800s, record the story of the Great Plains Indians' buffalo hunt, including the folklore and customs involved.				

Focus: B—Biography and autobiography; **C**—Collection of works; **H**—History; **S**—Story; **T**—Techniques or skills; **WC**—World cultures

Related discipline: D—Dance; **E–LA**—English–language arts; **H–SS**—History–social science; **MA**—Mathematics; **MU**—Music; **S**—Science; **TH**—Theatre; **VA**—Visual arts

Framework **component: AP**—Artistic perception; **AV**—Aesthetic valuing; **CE**—Creative expression; **HCC**—Historical and cultural context

✪ Denotes film or videotape

	Focus	Grade level	Related discipline	Framework component
✪ *Frida Kahlo.* n.d. Order from Arts America, 9 Benedict Place, Greenwich, CT 06830, (800) 553-5278. Frida Kahlo lived and worked at the center of the Mexican Renaissance in the 1920s and 1930s. A catastrophic accident at age sixteen left her with severe injuries. During her recuperation she began to paint complex works. The themes of death and her loss of motherhood inform her most powerful paintings.	B	9–12		AP HCC
Gardner, Jane Mylum. *Henry Moore: From Bones and Stones to Sketches and Sculptures.* New York: Four Winds, 1993. The author provides the reader with a unique opportunity to watch the sculptor at work. Black-and-white photographs illustrate the beauty of Henry Moore's sculptures.	B	K–3	H–SS	AP HCC
Gelber, Carol. *Masks Tell Stories.* Brookfield, Conn.: Millbrook, 1993. The author discusses the uses of masks in ancient societies' religious ceremonies, holiday celebrations, theatrical performances, and daily life.	WC	6–8	DR E–LA	HCC
Gibbons, Gail. *Lights! Camera! Action! How a Movie Is Made.* New York: HarperCollins, 1985. The author presents a step-by-step description of how a movie is made, including writing the script, casting, rehearsing, creating the scenery and costumes, editing the film, and attending the premiere. The colorful illustrations add verve to the text.	S	K–3	E–LA DR	AP
Gilow, Louise. *Meet Jim Henson.* New York: Random House, 1993. The creator of the Muppets, puppet stars of television and the movies, is the subject of this biography.	B	6–8	E–LA DR	AP HCC
Glubok, Shirley. *The Art of Ancient Peru.* New York: Harper and Row, 1976. This is a well-illustrated account of the Incas and many other civilizations in Peru whose art dates back about 2,500 years before the fall of the Incas. See also Glubok's *The Art of Ancient Peru, The Art of China,* and *The Art of the New American Nation.*	WC	9–12	H–SS	HCC
Goble, Paul. *The Girl Who Loved Wild Horses.* New York: Macmillan (Aladdin), 1986. A village girl who understands horses in a special way vanishes with a wild herd. When she is returned to her tribe, she becomes ill, until she is allowed to return to live with the wild horses.	S	4–5	H–SS	AP AV

Focus: **B**—Biography and autobiography; **C**—Collection of works; **H**—History; **S**—Story; **T**—Techniques or skills; **WC**—World cultures
Related discipline: **D**—Dance; **E–LA**—English–language arts; **H–SS**—History–social science; **MA**—Mathematics; **MU**—Music; **S**—Science; **TH**—Theatre; **VA**—Visual arts
Framework **component:** **AP**—Artistic perception; **AV**—Aesthetic valuing; **CE**—Creative expression; **HCC**—Historical and cultural context

✪ Denotes film or videotape

	Focus	Grade level	Related discipline	Framework component
Gonen, Rirka. *Fired Up! Making Pottery in Ancient Times.* Minneapolis, Minn.: Lerner, 1993.	WC	6–8	H–SS	HCC
This is an illustrated discussion of how pottery was made and used in ancient times and how archaeologists use these vessels today to learn about the past.				
Greene, Katherine, and Richard Greene. *The Man Behind the Magic: The Story of Walt Disney.* New York: Viking, 1991.	B	6–8	H–SS	HCC
This biography of Walt Disney discusses his boyhood on a Missouri farm, his struggles as a young animator, and his building of a motion picture and amusement park empire.				
Guback, Georgia. *Luka's Quilt.* New York: Greenwillow, 1994.	S	4–5	H–SS	HCC
When Luka's grandmother prepares to make a traditional Hawaiian quilt for her, they disagree over the colors it should include.				
Harns, Nathaniel. *Leonardo and the Renaissance.* *Time-Life* series. New York: Bookwright, 1987.	H B	9–12	H–SS	HCC
The Renaissance and Leonardo da Vinci's work during that period of history are described in this volume of the *Time-Life* series of biographies of artists.				
Hastings, Selina. *The Firebird.* New York: Candlewick, 1993.	S	4–5	E–LA	AP
This retelling of an East European fairy tale, originally researched and collected by the nineteenth-century folklorist A. F. Afanasyev, is a tale of the troubles that beset a huntsman who discovers a feather of the magic firebird. The illustrations by Regina Cartwright provide good examples of the use of color.				
Hathaway, Nancy. *Native American Portraits, 1862–1918: Photographs from the Collection of Kurt Koegler.* San Francisco: Chronicle Books, 1990.	H	9–12	H–SS	HCC
Portraits of Native Americans document the decline of indigenous civilizations in the late nineteenth century. This account provides an interesting perspective by using photography to document art and culture.				
Hernandez, Xavier, and Pilar Comes. *Barmi: A Mediterranean City Through the Ages.* Houghton Mifflin, 1990.	H	9–12	H–SS	HCC
The authors trace the development of a fictitious Mediterranean city whose characteristics are based on the cities of the southern Mediterranean coast. Jordi Ballouga illustrates this book, which could be used in a study of art history or architecture.				

Focus: B—Biography and autobiography; **C**—Collection of works; **H**—History; **S**—Story; **T**—Techniques or skills; **WC**—World cultures
Related discipline: D—Dance; **E–LA**—English–language arts; **H–SS**—History–social science; **MA**—Mathematics; **MU**—Music; **S**—Science; **TH**—Theatre; **VA**—Visual arts
Framework **component: AP**—Artistic perception; **AV**—Aesthetic valuing; **CE**—Creative expression; **HCC**—Historical and cultural context

✪ Denotes film or videotape

	Focus	Grade level	Related discipline	Framework component
Heslewood, Juliet. *Introducing Picasso: Painter, Sculptor.* Boston: Little, Brown, 1993. By examining the life of the well-known modern painter and the historical and artistic influences on his work, young readers get a sense of who he was and how his art developed. Photographs illustrate his work and his life.	B	6–8	H–SS	HCC AV
Hru, Dakari. *Joshua's Masai Mask.* New York: Lee and Low, 1993. Fearing that his classmates will ridicule his playing the kalimba in the school talent show, Joshua uses a magical Masai mask to transform himself into different people he thinks are more interesting. He comes to realize that his own identity is valuable.	S	6–8	H–SS MU	HCC AV
An Illustrated Anthology of Poems for Young People: Talking to the Sun. Selected and introduced by Kenneth Koch and Kate Farrell. New York: Metropolitan Museum of Art and Henry Holt, 1985. This collection matches poetry from ancient to modern cultures around the world to works of art found in the Metropolitan Museum of Art.	C	6–8	H–SS	AP CE
"Introduction to the Renaissance," *Calliope: World History for Young People.* Peterborough, N.H.: Cobblestone Publishing, May/June, 1994. This issue of *Calliope* deals with many aspects of the arts and sciences during the Italian Renaissance. It features articles on artists such as Michelangelo and Leonardo da Vinci, rulers such as Isabella d'Este, and composers such as Monteverdi.	H	6–8	H–SS MU	HCC
Isaacson, Philip M. *Round Buildings, Square Buildings and Buildings That Wiggle like a Fish.* New York: Knopf, 1988. The author examines the history and significance of an array of buildings, from ancient to contemporary times. This book is beautifully written and illustrated with color photographs. See also Isaacson's *A Short Walk Around the Pyramids* and *Through the World of Art.*	H	4–5	H–SS	AP HCC
Johnston, Tony, and Tomie DePaola. *The Quilt Story.* New York: Putnam, 1985. This story is about a frontier girl's patchwork quilt and its transformation through generations of one family.	S	6–8	E–LA	HCC AV

Focus: B—Biography and autobiography; **C**—Collection of works; **H**—History; **S**—Story; **T**—Techniques or skills; **WC**—World cultures
Related discipline: D—Dance; **E–LA**—English–language arts; **H–SS**—History–social science; **MA**—Mathematics; **MU**—Music; **S**—Science; **TH**—Theatre; **VA**—Visual arts
Framework **component: AP**—Artistic perception; **AV**—Aesthetic valuing; **CE**—Creative expression; **HCC**—Historical and cultural context

⊙ Denotes film or videotape

	Focus	Grade level	Related discipline	Framework component
Johnston, Tony. *The Last Snow of Winter.* New York: Tambourine, 1993.	S	6–8	E–LA	AV
The great sculptor Gaston Pompicard creates a snow sculpture for his friends. Later, he receives a similar gift from them during the last snow of winter. Watercolors and ink drawings by Frisco Heustra illustrate.				
Jonas, Ann. *Round Trip.* New York: Greenwillow, 1983.	S	K–3	S.	AP
The author leads a journey through a neighborhood, factories, and cities, teaching a lesson on positive and negative space and the creation of illusion.				
Kalman, Maira. *Max in Hollywood, Baby.* New York: Viking, 1993.	S	6–8	E–LA	AP AV
Max, the millionaire dog-poet, and his Parisian dalmatian friend, Crepes Suzette, leave Paris for the lure of glittering Hollywood. Can movie stardom be far behind?				
Kaplan, Andrew. *Careers for Artistic Types.* Brookfield, Conn.: Millbrook, 1991.	B	6–8		HCC
The author interviews 14 people who work in careers that are interesting to young people who like art.				
Kastner, Joseph. *John James Audubon.* New York: Harry Abrams, 1992.	B	6–8	H–SS	HCC
This biography chronicles the life of Audubon, from his childhood in France to his adventures in the New World, and shows how he captured these adventures in his artwork.				
Kehoe, Michael. *A Book Takes Root: The Making of a Picture Book.* Minneapolis, Minn.: Carolrhoda, 1993.	S	6–8	E–LA	AP CE
This book traces the process of making a picture book, from idea to manuscript to final production. Color photographs accompany the text and make this a fun-to-read and informative book.				
Krull, Kathleen. *Alex Fitzgerald, TV Star.* Boston: Little, Brown, 1991.	S	4–5	E–LA	AP
Alex's new fourth grade friendships in California are endangered when her chance to appear in a music video brings her glamour and an inflated ego.				
Kuskin, Karla. *Patchwork Island.* New York: HarperCollins, 1994.	S	K–3	E–LA	AP
A mother stitches a patchwork quilt for her child using the shapes and images of the varied landscape of their beautiful island. The vivid illustrations of Petra Mathews enhance the story. See also Kuskin's *City Noise* and *Paul,* which includes paintings by Milton Avery.				

Focus: B—Biography and autobiography; **C**—Collection of works; **H**—History; **S**—Story; **T**—Techniques or skills; **WC**—World cultures
Related discipline: D—Dance; **E–LA**—English–language arts; **H–SS**—History–social science; **MA**—Mathematics; **MU**—Music; **S**—Science; **TH**—Theatre; **VA**—Visual arts
***Framework* component: AP**—Artistic perception; **AV**—Aesthetic valuing; **CE**—Creative expression; **HCC**—Historical and cultural context

🔾 Denotes film or videotape

	Focus	Grade level	Related discipline	Framework component
Latkin, Patricia. *The Palace of Stars.* New York: Tambourine, 1993. After many Saturday outings at the expense of her great-uncle Max, Amanda takes him for a surprise visit to what she calls the palace of stars. The illustrations by Kimberly Bulcken Root enhance the text.	S	4–5	E–LA	AV
Lawrence, Jacob. *The Great Migration.* New York: HarperCollins, 1993. A series of paintings chronicles the journey of African Americans who, like the artist's family, left the rural South in the early twentieth century to find a better life in the industrial North. Included are paintings by Jacob Lawrence and a poem by Walter Dean Myers.	S	6–8	H–SS	HCC
Lazo, Caroline. *The Terra Cotta Army of Emperor Qin.* New York: Macmillan, 1993. Lazo describes the discovery of the great clay army buried near the tomb of China's Emperor Qin. Photographs of the objects are included.	WC	9–12	H–SS	HCC
Lehan, Daniel. *This Is Not a Book About Dodos.* Dutton, 1992. A landscape artist is dismayed when a flock of dodos appears on a mountain he is painting. Eventually he learns to incorporate them into his artwork.	S	K–3	E–LA	AP
Lemieux, Michele (retold and illustrated by the author). *Peter and the Wolf: Story by Sergei Prokofiev.* New York: Morrow Junior Books, 1991. Prokofiev wrote and orchestrated this tale to teach children about the instruments in an orchestra. The author vividly illustrates this retelling.	S	K–3	E–LA	AP
Levine, Arthur A. *The Boy Who Drew Cats.* New York: Penguin, 1993. An artistic young boy's love for drawing cats gets him into trouble that leads to a mysterious experience. Luminous paintings and calligraphy enhance and complement the story, which is based on a Japanese legend.	S	6–8	E–LA	HCC AV
Levitin, Sonja. *The Man Who Kept His Heart in a Bucket.* New York: Dial, 1991. Having once had his heart broken, Jack keeps it in a bucket, safe from harm, until one day a young maiden asks him to solve a riddle which teaches him the true meaning of love. The watercolor illustrations are by Jerry Pinkney.	S	4–5	E–LA	AP

Focus: **B**—Biography and autobiography; **C**—Collection of works; **H**—History; **S**—Story; **T**—Techniques or skills; **WC**—World cultures
Related discipline: **D**—Dance; **E–LA**—English–language arts; **H–SS**—History–social science; **MA**—Mathematics; **MU**—Music; **S**—Science; **TH**—Theatre; **VA**—Visual arts
Framework component: **AP**—Artistic perception; **AV**—Aesthetic valuing; **CE**—Creative expression; **HCC**—Historical and cultural context

○ Denotes film or videotape

	Focus	Grade level	Related discipline	Framework component
Lewis, Naomi. *Hans Christian Andersen's The Snow Queen.* Cambridge, Mass.: Candlewick, 1993. After the Snow Queen abducts her friend Kan, Gerda sets out on a perilous and magical journey to find him. The illustrations in watercolor and pencil are by Angela Barrett and beautifully illustrate the text.	S	4–5	E–LA	AP
Lionni, Leo. *Little Blue and Little Yellow.* New York: Ivan Obolensky, 1991. Blue and Yellow, torn-paper "figures," journey together through various experiences, eventually joining to make Green.	S	K–3	E–LA	AP CE
Livingston, Myra Cohn. *Light and Shadow.* New York: Holiday House, 1992. Poems about the viewing of light in different settings are accompanied by beautiful photographs.	T	4–5	S	AP
Llorente, Pilar Molina. *The Apprentice.* Translated by Robin Longshaw. New York: Farrar, Straus and Giroux, 1993. In Renaissance Florence, thirteen-year-old Arduino dreams of becoming a painter as an apprentice to renowned artist Cosimo di Forli. When Arduino discovers that a talented pupil has been secretly imprisoned in the attic, he realizes to what lengths artistic jealously has driven the maestro.	S	4–5	E–LA	HCC AV
Lobel, Arnold. *The Great Blueness and Other Predicaments.* New York: HarperCollins, 1968. This book tells the story of the Wizard, who lives in a gray world. When he discovers the color blue, he turns the world blue. The people are happy until so much blue turns everyone sad. Then the wizard discovers yellow, and the people are happy until too much of this color hurts everyone's eyes. At last Wizard finds a way to make the world so beautiful it never needs to be changed. See also Lobel's *Martha the Movie Mouse*.	S	4–5	E–LA	AP AV
Locker, Thomas. *Sailing with the Wind.* New York: Dial, 1986. Land, water, and sky change constantly as a young girl sails to an ocean she has never seen. When she returns home, she has had a taste of the splendor and mystery of the wider world.	S	4–5	E–LA	AP
Lund, Jillian. *Way Out West Lives a Coyote Named Frank.* New York: Dutton, 1993. The author uses vibrant colors to tell the tale of a coyote named Frank and his adventures in the desert.	S	K–3		AP CE

Focus: B—Biography and autobiography; **C**—Collection of works; **H**—History; **S**—Story; **T**—Techniques or skills; **WC**—World cultures
Related discipline: D—Dance; **E–LA**—English–language arts; **H–SS**—History–social science; **MA**—Mathematics; **MU**—Music; **S**—Science; **TH**—Theatre; **VA**—Visual arts
***Framework* component: AP**—Artistic perception; **AV**—Aesthetic valuing; **CE**—Creative expression; **HCC**—Historical and cultural context

◐ Denotes film or videotape

	Focus	Grade level	Related discipline	Framework component
Lyons, Mary E. *Deep Blues: Bill Traylor, Self-Taught Artist.* New York: Scribner's, 1994.	B	6–8	H–SS	HCC
This is a biography of the twentieth-century African-American folk artist. It is part of the *AFRICAN-AMERICAN ARTISTS AND ARTISANS* series and is richly illustrated with photographs of Traylor's works. See also Lyons's *Master of Mahogany: Tom Day, Free Black Cabinet Maker; Stitching Stars: The Story Quilts of Harriet Powers;* and *Starting Home: The Story of Horace Pippin, Painter.*				
Macaulay, David. *City: A Story of Roman Planning and Construction.* Boston: Houghton Mifflin, 1990.	H	9–12	H–SS	HCC
The author discusses the Romans' methods of planning and constructing their cities for the people who lived in them. Beautiful pen-and-ink illustrations demonstrate a rich use of perspective techniques.				
MacClintock, Dorcas. *Animals Observed: A Look at Animals in Art.* New York: Scribner's, 1993.	C	4–5	H–SS	HCC
This collection of drawings, paintings, and sculptures depicts a variety of animals, including giraffes, elephants, zebras, squirrels, dogs, cats, and horses. The author discusses the artists and the animals they have observed.				
McDermott, Gerald. *Arrow to the Sun.* Puffin, 1986.	WC	K–3	H–SS	HCC
This Caldecott Award book concerns an Indian boy's transformation into an arrow that reaches heaven and returns to earth. The illustrations are graphic shapes that fit the text and theme.				
McHugh, Christopher. *DISCOVERING ART* series. *Water.* New York: Thompson Learning, 1993.	H	4–5	H–SS	HCC
In this collection of paintings, old and new, water is the central theme. The author provides a short biographical sketch of each artist and a glossary pertinent to history and art history. The same format is used for the rest of the books in this series: *Animals, Faces, Food, People at Work,* and *Town and Country.*				
Madison, Jon. *Beautiful Junk.* Boston: Little, Brown, 1968.	B	6–8	E–LA	AP HCC
This story of how Simon Rodia built the Watts Towers is told from the point of view of two neighborhood boys.				
Maxuer, Joyce. *Lady Bugatti.* New York: Lothrop, Lee and Shepard, 1991.	S	K–3	E–LA	AP
The author and artist Kevin Hawkes tell the tale, in verse, of Lady Bugatti and her fellow critters and their adventurous and colorful evening at the theatre.				

Focus: B—Biography and autobiography; **C**—Collection of works; **H**—History; **S**—Story; **T**—Techniques or skills; **WC**—World cultures
Related discipline: D—Dance; **E–LA**—English-language arts; **H–SS**—History–social science; **MA**—Mathematics; **MU**—Music; **S**—Science; **TH**—Theatre; **VA**—Visual arts
Framework **component: AP**—Artistic perception; **AV**—Aesthetic valuing; **CE**—Creative expression; **HCC**—Historical and cultural context

○ Denotes film or videotape

	Focus	Grade level	Related discipline	Framework component
Mayers, Florence Cassell. *ABC.* New York: Harry Abrams, 1988.	C	K–3	E–LA	HCC
The author illustrates the letters of the alphabet with artwork from the Museum of Modern Art, New York; the Brooklyn Museum; the Museum of Fine Arts, Boston; and the National Air and Space Museum, Washington, D.C.				
Mickelthwait, Lucy. *A Child's Book of Art: Great Pictures, First Words.* London: Dorling Kindersley, 1993.	H	K–3		HCC AV
The author introduces art to very young children using well-known works of art from around the world to illustrate familiar words. Sections include "Things to Do," "Pets," and "The Seasons." The artists represented range from Hiroshige to Toulouse-Lautrec, from Caravaggio to Hans Hoffman. See also Mickelthwait's *I Spy: An Alphabet in Art; I Spy a Lion: Animals in Art;* and *I Spy Two Eyes: Numbers in Art.*				
Monceaux, Morgan. *Jazz: My Music, My People.* New York: Knopf, 1994.	B	4–5	MU	H–CC
Short biographies, accompanied by vibrant portraits by Monceaux, make this an easy-to-read history of jazz. The illustrations could be used in a visual arts class as models for the expressive use of line and color.				
Moss, Miriam. *Fashion World: Fashion Designer.* New York: Macmillan, 1991.	T	4–5		AP
A glimpse into the creative world of the fashion designer shows how new styles are conceived, produced, and marketed. See also Moss's *Fashion World: Fashion Photographer.*				
✪ *Mountain in the Mind.* The Minneapolis Institute of Arts, n.d. Order from Arts America, 9 Benedict Place, Greenwich, CT 06830, (800) 553-5278.	B	9–12		AP HCC
In this video, noted Hong Kong artist Wucius Wong explains the traditional Chinese approach to landscape painting: the need to create both the essence of nature and the emotion of the artist in contemplating it. The camera follows Wong closely as he visits a familiar Minnesota landmark, Minnehaha Falls, and then paints it later from memory in his studio.				
Muhlberger, Richard. *What Makes a Degas a Degas?* New York: Viking and the Metropolitan Museum of Art, 1993.	H	9–12	H–SS	HCC
The author explores such art topics as style, composition, color, and subject matter as they relate to the works of Degas. Other volumes in the series discuss Raphael, Rembrandt, van Gogh, Bruegel, and Monet.				

Focus: **B**—Biography and autobiography; **C**—Collection of works; **H**—History; **S**—Story; **T**—Techniques or skills; **WC**—World cultures
Related discipline: **D**—Dance; **E–LA**—English–language arts; **H–SS**—History–social science; **MA**—Mathematics; **MU**—Music; **S**—Science;
   TH—Theatre; **VA**—Visual arts
Framework **component:** **AP**—Artistic perception; **AV**—Aesthetic valuing; **CE**—Creative expression; **HCC**—Historical and cultural context

✪ Denotes film or videotape

	Focus	Grade level	Related discipline	Framework component

Neimark, Anne E. *Diego Rivera: Artist of the People.* HarperCollins, 1992.

> Diego Rivera is brought to life in this comprehensive biography. It is illustrated with reproductions of Rivera's artwork.

H B — 6–8 — H–SS — HCC

Newlands, Anne. *Meet Edgar Degas.* New York: Lippincott, 1988.

> Degas talks to the reader about each of 13 paintings, describing what it's like to be a young artist in Paris.

H B — 6–8 — H–SS — HCC

Oram, Hiawyn. *Out of the Blue: Poems About Color.* New York: Hyperion, 1993.

> The theme of this collection of poems is color. Titles include "Red Tape," "Sacred Yellow," "Gray Heads," and "The Green-Eyed Monster." Illustrations by David McKee complement the text.

C — K–3 — E–LA — AP

Parton, Dolly. *Coat of Many Colors.* New York: HarperCollins, 1994.

> A poor girl delights in her coat of many colors, made by her mother from rags. Despite the ridicule of the other children, she knows the coat was made with love. The story is illustrated with colorful paintings by Judith Sutton.

S — 4–5 — MU — AV

Paul, Anne Whitford. *Eight Hands Round: A Patchwork Alphabet.* New York: HarperCollins, 1991.

> The author introduces the letters of the alphabet through Early American patchwork quilt patterns. She explains the origins of the designs by describing the activity or occupation they derive from.

H — K–3 — H–SS — AP

Paulsen, Gary. *The Monument.* New York: Delacorte, 1991.

> Thirteen-year-old Rocky has her life changed by the remarkable artist who comes to her small Kansas town to design a war memorial.

S — 9–12 — E–LA — AV

Pekarik, Andrew. *Painting: Behind the Scenes.* New York: Hyperion, 1992.

> Pekarik discusses the principles of color, line, and perspective in painting. The author also wrote *Sculpture: Behind the Scenes* (in association with the PBS series).

T — 9–12 — — AP

Perlman, Marc. *Movie Classics.* Minneapolis, Minn.: Lerner, 1993.

> The author describes and analyzes seven classic movies, from *Metropolis* to *Annie Hall,* and places them in the context of cinema history.

H — 9–12 — H–SS — HCC

Focus: B—Biography and autobiography; **C**—Collection of works; **H**—History; **S**—Story; **T**—Techniques or skills; **WC**—World cultures
Related discipline: D—Dance; **E–LA**—English-language arts; **H–SS**—History–social science; **MA**—Mathematics; **MU**—Music; **S**—Science; **TH**—Theatre; **VA**—Visual arts
Framework **component: AP**—Artistic perception; **AV**—Aesthetic valuing; **CE**—Creative expression; **HCC**—Historical and cultural context

◐ Denotes film or videotape

	Focus	Grade level	Related discipline	Framework component
Pinkwater, Daniel M. *The Big Orange Splot*. New York: Scholastic, 1977.	S	K–3	E–LA	AP AV
Mr. Plumbean lived on a street where all the houses were the same color (very boring) until a seagull dropped a can of orange paint on his house. The story follows the transformation of the neighborhood into one of unique houses.				
Platt, Richard. *EYEWITNESS BOOKS* series. *Film*. New York: Knopf, 1992.	H	9–12	H–SS	AP HCC
This history of film is examined through photographs, art, and tools of the film industry. The *EYEWITNESS* series provides an in-depth look at many topics in art and science.				
Polacco, Patricia. *Chicken Sunday*. New York: Philomel, 1992.	WC	K–3	H–SS	HCC
Three children decorate Easter eggs in the Ukraine tradition and earn money to buy Miss Eula a beautiful Easter hat.				
Raboff, Ernest. *ART FOR CHILDREN* series. New York: Harper and Row, 1988.	H B	K–3	H–SS	HCC
This series, which includes books on Velasquez, Remington, Toulouse-Lautrec, Picasso, Raphael, Gauguin, Paul Klee, Chagall, van Gogh, Rousseau, Rembrandt, da Vinci, Renoir, Michelangelo, Matisse, and Dürer, presents brief biographies of the artists, coupled with reproductions and brief analyses of their work.				
Richmond, Robin. *Introducing Michelangelo*. New York: Little, Brown, 1991.	H	4–5	H–SS	HCC
In this biography readers will learn the details of the commission of Michelangelo to paint the Sistine Chapel. The author also discusses the chapel's recent restoration. Examples of Michelangelo's work complement the text.				
Ringgold, Faith. *Aunt Harriet's Underground Railroad in the Sky*. New York: Crown, 1992.	S	K–3	E–LA	HCC
With Harriet Tubman as her guide, Cassie retraces the route that escaping slaves took on the Underground Railroad, hoping to unite with her younger brother. Ringgold's paintings are strong and provide a look at an artist who has assurance and control over her medium. See also Ringgold's *Dinner at Aunt Connie's House* and *Tar Beach*.				
Roalf, Peggy. *LOOKING AT PAINTINGS* series. *Dancers*. New York: Hyperion, 1992.	H	4–5	H–SS	AP HCC
All aspects of dance are captured in this history of dance in art. The artists represented range from ancient to contemporary. Other titles in the series include *Horses, Families, Seascapes, Cats, Landscapes,* and *Self-Portraits*.				

Focus: **B**—Biography and autobiography; **C**—Collection of works; **H**—History; **S**—Story; **T**—Techniques or skills; **WC**—World cultures
Related discipline: **D**—Dance; **E–LA**—English–language arts; **H–SS**—History–social science; **MA**—Mathematics; **MU**—Music; **S**—Science; **TH**—Theatre; **VA**—Visual arts
Framework **component:** **AP**—Artistic perception; **AV**—Aesthetic valuing; **CE**—Creative expression; **HCC**—Historical and cultural context

🔾 Denotes film or videotape

	Focus	Grade level	Related discipline	Framework component
Roth, Roger. *The Sign Painter's Dream.* New York: Crown, 1993. A spunky old woman's request and a rather unusual dream convince Crabby Clarence, the sign painter, to make the most glorious and magnificent sign of his career and then give it away. Roth's watercolor illustrations enhance the story.	S	4–5	E–LA	AP AV
Roth, Susan L. *Gypsy Bird Song.* New York: Farrar, Straus and Giroux, 1991. "Whenever you see a gypsy bird, it means the Gypsies are near." With this promise, readers are led by the gypsy bird through a riot of color and poetry to the magical world of the Gypsies.	S	K–3	E–LA	AP
Rowland-Warne, L. EYEWITNESS BOOKS series. *Costumes.* New York: Knopf, 1992. This informational book examines costumes throughout history. Illustrations include photographs, drawings, and works of art.	H	6–8	H–SS	HCC
Rylant, Cynthia. *Something Permanent.* Photographs by Walker Evans. San Diego, Calif.: Harcourt Brace, 1994. The photographs of Walker Evans tell stories of ordinary people living in America in the extraordinary time of the Great Depression. The poems of Cynthia Rylant project a new voice in this telling—a voice at once reverent and clear. The photographs and poems are linked in beautiful and visionary ways.	C	9–12	E–LA	HCC AV
Sayer, Chloe. *Arts and Crafts of Mexico.* San Francisco: Chronicle Books, 1990. This beautifully wrought history of Mexican arts and crafts focuses on contemporary work but provides a foundation for work done in the past.	H	9–12	H–SS	HCC
Scott, Elaine. *Funny Papers: Behind the Scenes of the Comics.* New York: William Morrow, 1993. This historical survey of comic strips examines different kinds and discusses how they are created and marketed. There are many illustrations of comic strips and interviews with the artists.	H	6–8	E–LA	AP HCC
Scott, Elaine. *Look Alive.* New York: Morrow Junior Books, 1992. This book describes the preproduction, production, and postproduction of animation, television movies, and specials through Beverly Cleary's character Ralph.	H	6–8	E–LA	AP HCC

Focus: B—Biography and autobiography; **C**—Collection of works; **H**—History; **S**—Story; **T**—Techniques or skills; **WC**—World cultures
Related discipline: D—Dance; **E–LA**—English-language arts; **H–SS**—History-social science; **MA**—Mathematics; **MU**—Music; **S**—Science; **TH**—Theatre; **VA**—Visual arts
Framework **component: AP**—Artistic perception; **AV**—Aesthetic valuing; **CE**—Creative expression; **HCC**—Historical and cultural context

🔵 Denotes film or videotape

	Focus	Grade level	Related discipline	Framework component
Sills, Leslie. *Inspirations: Stories About Women Artists.* New York: Albert Whitman, 1989.	B	9–12	H–SS	HCC
Unique visions of artists Georgia O'Keefe, Frida Kahlo, Alice Neel, and Faith Ringgold are shown through the lives and art of these four women who lived and worked in the twentieth century.				
Skofield, James. *Round and Around.* New York: HarperCollins, 1993.	S	4–5	S	AP
A little boy and his father go for a walk and find circular shapes in everything they see and do. Luminous watercolor and pencil illustrations by James Graham Hale accompany the text.				
Staines, Bill. *River.* New York: Penguin, 1994.	S	4–5	MU	AV CE
Expressionist paintings by Kate Spohn illustrate Staines's song "River." They reflect a young person's musings on the progress of life as symbolized by the flow of the river.				
Stanley, Diane. *The Gentleman and the Kitchen Maid.* New York: Penguin, 1994.	S	6–8	DR	AP AV
When the subjects in two paintings hanging across from each other in a museum fall in love, a resourceful art student finds a way to unite the lovers. This story is an excellent discussion starter and entry into the art world.				
Staskowski, Andrea. *Movie Musicals.* Minneapolis, Minn.: Lerner, 1992.	H	6–8	DR	HCC
This book discusses the musical film genre and gives analysis and plot summaries of several notable musicals, such as *Top Hat, Meet Me in St. Louis, Grease,* and *Dirty Dancing.*				
Steptoe, John. *Mufaro's Beautiful Daughters: An African Tale.* New York: Lothrop, Lee and Shepard, 1987.	WC	K–3	H–SS	HCC
Mufaro sends his daughter on a journey to appear before the Great King, who wants a wife. A series of incidents and unusual choices make her queen.				
Sturgis, Alexander. *Introducing Rembrandt.* Boston: Little, Brown, 1994.	H B	4–5	H–SS	HCC AV
Sturgis explores Rembrandt's painting and editing techniques and examines how changing political and social fashions in Amsterdam affected the artist's career. The author also discusses the problems in authenticating Rembrandt's work.				
Sufrin, Mark. *George Catlin: Painter of the Indian West.* New York: Atheneum, 1991.	B	6–8	H–SS	HCC
This account of the Pennsylvania-born artist whose desire was to capture the remnants of a dying civilization includes many reproductions of Catlin's work.				

Focus: **B**—Biography and autobiography; **C**—Collection of works; **H**—History; **S**—Story; **T**—Techniques or skills; **WC**—World cultures
Related discipline: **D**—Dance; **E–LA**—English–language arts; **H–SS**—History–social science; **MA**—Mathematics; **MU**—Music; **S**—Science; **TH**—Theatre; **VA**—Visual arts
***Framework* component:** **AP**—Artistic perception; **AV**—Aesthetic valuing; **CE**—Creative expression; **HCC**—Historical and cultural context

◐ Denotes film or videotape

	Focus	Grade level	Related discipline	Framework component
Sullivan, George. *Matthew Brady: His Life and Photographs.* New York: Cobblehill Books, 1994.	B	9–12	H–SS	HCC
In photography's very early days, Brady realized that photographs could provide a visual record of people and events. He and his studio assistants photographed most of the celebrated figures of the time. This book documents Brady's life and is richly illustrated with photographs.				
Sutcliff, Rosemary. *Chess-Dream in a Garden.* Cambridge, Mass.: Candlewick, 1993.	S	4–5	E–LA	AP
Set in a garden, this is the tale of the White King and his Queen. Served by their Bishops, Knights, and humble Pawns, they live in peace until, one day, jealousy opens the garden wall to their enemy, the Red Horde. Taking their positions on the checkered lawn, the Red and White companies begin to fight. The watercolor illustrations are superb.				
Sweentzell, Rina. *Children of Clay: A Family of Pueblo Potters.* Minneapolis, Minn.: Lerner, 1992.	WC	4–5	H–SS	HCC
Members of a Tewa Indian family living in Santa Clara Pueblo in New Mexico follow the age-old traditions of their people as they create various objects of clay. Color photographs of the family and the New Mexico landscape, as well as maps, accompany the text.				
Talking with Artists. Edited by Pat Cummings. New York: Bradbury, 1992.	B	9–12	DR	HCC
Fourteen distinguished picture-book illustrators talk about their early art experiences, answer questions most frequently asked by children, and offer encouragement to those who would like to become artists. Each artist's section features his or her illustrations.				
Turner, Robyn Montana. PORTRAITS OF WOMEN ARTISTS FOR CHILDREN series. *Rosa Bonheur.* New York: Little, Brown, 1992.	H B	4–5	H–SS	HCC
This biography chronicles the life of Rosa Bonheur, a nineteenth-century French sculptor and artist. She was known for her realistic portrayals of people, animals, and landscapes. Her body of work includes paintings of Buffalo Bill's troupe, made during its encampment near Paris. This series on women artists includes volumes on Mary Cassatt, Frida Kahlo, and Georgia O'Keefe.				

Focus: B—Biography and autobiography; **C**—Collection of works; **H**—History; **S**—Story; **T**—Techniques or skills; **WC**—World cultures
Related discipline: D—Dance; **E–LA**—English–language arts; **H–SS**—History–social science; **MA**—Mathematics; **MU**—Music; **S**—Science; **TH**—Theatre; **VA**—Visual arts
Framework **component: AP**—Artistic perception; **AV**—Aesthetic valuing; **CE**—Creative expression; **HCC**—Historical and cultural context

✪ Denotes film or videotape

	Focus	Grade level	Related discipline	Framework component
Van Allsburg, Chris. *The Polar Express.* Boston, Mass.: Houghton Mifflin, 1985. This Caldecott Medal winner is a holiday story about a boy's imaginary trip to the North Pole, his special experience with Santa, and the "bell" that only believers can hear. See also the author's *The Garden of Abdul Gasazi, The Mysteries of Harris Burdick,* and *Just a Dream.*	S	K–3	E–LA S	AP
Venezia, Mike. GETTING TO KNOW THE WORLD'S GREATEST ARTISTS series. *Picasso.* New York: Harper & Row, 1983. Illustrations by the author and Picasso's own work enhance this account of the artist's life. See also the author's books on da Vinci, Hopper, Monet, Rembrandt, van Gogh, Botticelli, Cassatt, and Goya.	H	K–3	H–SS	HCC
Waldman, Neil. *America the Beautiful.* New York: Macmillan, 1993. This is an illustrated edition of the nineteenth-century poem, later set to music, that celebrates the beauty of America. The acrylic paintings by Waldman are luminous landscapes.	C	4–5	H–SS	HCC
Walker, Lou Ann. *Roy Lichtenstein: The Artist at Work.* New York: Penguin, 1994. The author focuses on how the artist develops a painting from original idea to finished piece. The photographs of Lichtenstein in his studio illustrate his working process and the development of his ideas.	B	4–5		HCC
Wardlaw, Lee. *The Tales of Grandpa Cat.* New York: Dial, 1994. When his grandchildren come to visit him in his retirement community, Grandpa Cat entertains them with exciting tales about the exploits of various fellow residents, Billy the Kitten and Miss Kitty Hawk among them. The pen-and-ink and acrylic drawings by Ronald Searle are outstanding examples of illustration.	S	4–5	E–LA	AP
Warren, Scott S. *Cities in the Sand: The Ancient Civilizations of the Southwest.* San Francisco: Chronicle Books, 1992. This book discusses some of the things archaeologists have learned about the culture and art of three major groups of Indians that lived in the American Southwest: the Anasazi, the Hohokam, and the Mogollon.	WC	6–8	H–SS	HCC

Focus: **B**—Biography and autobiography; **C**—Collection of works; **H**—History; **S**—Story; **T**—Techniques or skills; **WC**—World cultures
Related discipline: **D**—Dance; **E–LA**—English–language arts; **H–SS**—History–social science; **MA**—Mathematics; **MU**—Music; **S**—Science; **TH**—Theatre; **VA**—Visual arts
Framework **component:** **AP**—Artistic perception; **AV**—Aesthetic valuing; **CE**—Creative expression; **HCC**—Historical and cultural context

◐ Denotes film or videotape

	Focus	Grade level	Related discipline	Framework component
Weiss, Harvey. *Cartoons and Cartooning.* New York: Houghton Mifflin, 1990.	T	6–8	E–LA	AP HCC
In this comprehensive guide to cartooning, the author covers its development as an art form and its uses and offers suggestions for young illustrators.				
Wells, Rosemary. *Night Sounds, Morning Colors.* New York: Dial, 1994.	S	4–5	E–LA	AP AV
A child explores the senses by reflecting on experiences associated with the seasons. The acrylic paintings by David McPhail invite the reader into the world described by Wells. This book could be used in both music and visual art lessons in which students explore the expressive uses of arts elements.				
Welton, Jude. *Drawing: A Young Artist's Guide.* London: Dorling Kindersley, 1994.	T	6–8		AP CE
This well-designed and beautifully illustrated book guides the young artist through a wide variety of artistic experiences. Each idea is illustrated with master drawings and paintings. Topics include light and shade, color, imagination, and storytelling.				
Westray, Kathleen. *A Color Sampler.* New York: Ticknor and Fields, 1993.	T	K–3		AP
The author discusses primary, secondary, and intermediate colors and shows how color is affected by its surroundings. The illustrations are adapted from classic patchwork quilt patterns.				
Willard, Nancy. *Pish, Posh, Said Hieronymus Bosch.* San Diego, Calif.: Harcourt Brace Jovanovich, 1991.	S	6–8	E–LA	HCC AV
In this imaginative poem about the household of fifteenth-century painter Hieronymus Bosch, the creatures Bosch paints come to life and vex the woman who takes care of the house. The vivid and delightful illustrations bring the text to life.				
Williams, Helen. *Stories in Art.* Brookfield, Conn.: Millbrook, 1991.	S	4–5	H–SS	AP HCC
The author draws from a variety of works, from ancient to contemporary, to illustrate how artists use stories in their works. Also see *Nature in Art, People in Art* and *Places in Art* from the same series.				
Williams, Karen Lynn. *Tap-Tap.* New York: Clarion, 1994.	S	4–5	E–LA	AP CE
After selling oranges in the market, a Haitian mother and daughter have enough money to ride the tap-tap, a truck that picks up passengers and lets them off when they bang on the side of the vehicle. The expressive watercolor paintings by Catherine Stock are excellent examples of book illustration.				

Focus: **B**—Biography and autobiography; **C**—Collection of works; **H**—History; **S**—Story; **T**—Techniques or skills; **WC**—World cultures
Related discipline: **D**—Dance; **E–LA**—English–language arts; **H–SS**—History–social science; **MA**—Mathematics; **MU**—Music; **S**—Science; **TH**—Theatre; **VA**—Visual arts
Framework **component:** **AP**—Artistic perception; **AV**—Aesthetic valuing; **CE**—Creative expression; **HCC**—Historical and cultural context

♦ Denotes film or videotape

	Focus	Grade level	Related discipline	Framework component
Williams, Neva. *Patrick des Jarlait: Conversations with a Native American Artist.* Minneapolis, Minn.: Lerner, 1994. Patrick des Jarlait was a well-known artist who devoted his talents to painting pictures of the lifeways of the Chippewa on Red Lake Indian Reservation in northern Minnesota. The text is from a series of taped interviews with the artist and is illustrated with des Jarlait's paintings and photographs of his life.	B	4–5	H–SS	HCC
Wilson, Elizabeth. *Bibles and Bestiaries: A Guide to Illuminated Manuscripts.* New York: The Pierpont Morgan Library, 1994. This history of illuminated books—that is, books or manuscripts that have been decorated with pictures to illustrate the text—shows the many ways the painting was done.	H	9–12	H–SS	HCC AV
Winter, Jonah. *Diego.* New York: Knopf, 1991. Winter tells the tale of Diego Rivera's childhood. An epilogue tells of his motivation to become an artist. The illustrations are beautifully done in a vibrant and modern style.	B	K–3	H–SS	HCC
Wolkstein, Diane. *Little Mouse's Painting.* New York: Morrow Junior Books, 1992. A little mouse's depiction of nature is enhanced by her own imagination and her friendship with a bear, a squirrel, and a porcupine.	S	K–3	E–LA	AP
Woolf, Felicity. *Picture This: A First Introduction to Paintings.* New York: Doubleday, 1989. This brief history of Western painting from the fifteenth century to the twentieth century includes reproductions. It is an informative introduction to the diversity and significance of Western painting.	H	4–5	H–SS	AP HCC
Woolfit, Gabrielle. *Colors* series. Minneapolis, Minn.: Carolrhoda, 1992. This series includes books titled *Green, Yellow, Blue,* and *Red.* Texts and photographs in each book describe familiar objects of the title's color.	T	K–3		AP
Yenawine, Philip. *Stories.* New York: The Museum of Modern Art/Delacorte, 1991. Works of modern art are used to introduce basic vocabulary and questions for aesthetic observation. See also Yenawine's *Colors.*	H	K–3	E–LA	AP HCC

Focus: **B**—Biography and autobiography; **C**—Collection of works; **H**—History; **S**—Story; **T**—Techniques or skills; **WC**—World cultures
Related discipline: **D**—Dance; **E–LA**—English–language arts; **H–SS**—History–social science; **MA**—Mathematics; **MU**—Music; **S**—Science; **TH**—Theatre; **VA**—Visual arts
Framework **component:** **AP**—Artistic perception; **AV**—Aesthetic valuing; **CE**—Creative expression; **HCC**—Historical and cultural context

● Denotes film or videotape

	Focus	Grade level	Related discipline	Framework component
Yesterday and Tomorrow: California Women Artists. Edited by Sylvia Moore. New York: Midmarch Arts, 1989.	H	9–12	H–SS	HCC
Essays by experts on topics such as the history of mural art, African-American art, Native-American art, the crafts of ceramics and quilting, and examples of the ethnic diversity of California art are included in this collection.				
Yorinks, Arthur. *Whitefish Will Rides Again!* New York: HarperCollins, 1994.	S	6–8	E–LA	AV
Whitefish Will was the mightiest lawman in the history of the Old West. But then the penny-pinching townsfolk put him out to pasture. So what happens when the meanest, rottenest, ugliest gang of outlaws steals all the horses, swipes everybody's clothes, and threatens to burn down the entire town? You guessed it? Whitefish Will rides again! Mort Drucker's drawings greatly enhance the story.				
Zhung, Zhensum, and Alice Lou. *A Young Painter: The Life and Paintings of Wang Yaui—China's Extraordinary Young Artist.* New York: Scholastic, 1991.	WC	4–5	H–SS	HCC
This book about a young Chinese artist traces her motivation to paint as a means of communication and as fulfillment of her creative inclinations. The author shows the development of the artist's style from childhood to adolescence.				

Focus: B—Biography and autobiography; **C**—Collection of works; **H**—History; **S**—Story; **T**—Techniques or skills; **WC**—World cultures
Related discipline: D—Dance; **E–LA**—English–language arts; **H–SS**—History–social science; **MA**—Mathematics; **MU**—Music; **S**—Science;
  TH—Theatre; **VA**—Visual arts
Framework **component: AP**—Artistic perception; **AV**—Aesthetic valuing; **CE**—Creative expression; **HCC**—Historical and cultural context

○ Denotes film or videotape

95-26 003-0078-95 300 1-96 1M